Landon Carter: An Inquiry

Landon Carter

An Inquiry into
the Personal Values and
Social Imperatives
of the Eighteenth-Century
Virginia Gentry

Jack P. Greene

The University Press of Virginia
Charlottesville

Copyrighted © 1965 by the Virginia
Historical Society as the Introduction to
*The Diary of Colonel Landon Carter of
Sabine Hall, 1752—1778,* edited by Jack P.
Greene. Slightly revised, the Introduction
is now issued separately under the present title.

First separate publication 1967

Fourth printing   1988

The University Press of Virginia

Library of Congress Catalog Card Number:
64—19201

Printed in the United States of America

Merui, sed intus
tantum fruor.

In spite of my merit,
I have only
inward satisfaction.

Preface

EXCEPT for a few minor changes in wording and
citations and the addition of a brief epilogue, this book
is simply a reprint of the Introduction to *The Diary
of Colonel Landon Carter of Sabine Hall, 1752–1776*
(2 vols., Charlottesville: University Press of Virginia,
1965). It had then and has now three intimately related
objectives. First, and most obviously, it is intended as
a plausible psychological and intellectual portrait of
Landon Carter, an effort to delineate his central
character traits and personal values; to call attention to
some of the things that motivated him; to determine
what major problems he encountered, how he sought
to solve them, and how well he succeeded; and to analyze
his responses to the major public events of his life—in
short, to look at his world in much the way as he must
have seen it. Second, and, from my point of view,
vastly more important, it is presented as an inquiry
into the personal values and social imperatives of the
eighteenth-century Virginia gentry, as an attempt to
identify through Carter the ideas and assumptions
that gave structure and coherence to both the private
and public worlds of that extraordinary group. Finally,
if largely only implicitly, it is offered as a case study
in the relationship between individual and collective
psychology and of the ways individual, even highly
idiosyncratic and partially antisocial, behavior may
illuminate broader social values. What it is not intended
to do and what can only be done by a lengthy series

of comparative investigations is to determine which, if any, of the largely traditional values held by Carter and the gentry received a special or peculiar emphasis that helped to distinguish Carter from other individuals or the gentry from other comparable groups in the eighteenth century.

Among the several individuals whose aid I acknowledged in the Preface to the diary and whose assistance in preparing this essay must be mentioned again here are W. W. Abbot, Keith B. Berwick, Robert M. Calhoon, Charles R. Crowe, Emory G. Evans, Norman S. Grabo, Sue N. Greene, Winthrop D. Jordan, Frank Rosengarten, Jean Paul Smith, and Thad W. Tate, Jr., all of whom read and criticized the original introduction, and Francis R. Bliss and Donald R. Laing, Jr., who helped in identifying and assessing the importance of the classical allusions in Carter's writings. Marvin B. Becker requires special thanks for helping over the past eight years to sharpen my understanding of the possibilities and importance of this kind of historical enterprise.

J. P. G.

Baltimore, Maryland
November 30, 1966

Contents

Landon Carter: An Inquiry

I Vita

Few children in colonial America were born with greater advantages than Landon Carter. His father, Robert "King" Carter, was one of the wealthiest Americans of his generation and perhaps the most prominent and most successful of that remarkable group that rose to dominance in Virginia during the last decades of the seventeenth century and provided the foundations for the famous Virginia gentry of the eighteenth century. By the time Landon— his fourth son, the third by his second wife, Elizabeth Landon Willis—was born on August 18, 1710, King Carter was already one of the most commanding figures in the colony, distinguished both by his enormous wealth and by a political career that stretched back over three decades and included service as justice of the peace for Lancaster County, vestryman in Christ Church Parish, speaker of the House of Burgesses, treasurer, and councilor. As agent for the Northern Neck proprietary after 1703, King Carter added those quantities of land to his already extensive holdings that would total some 333,000 acres at his death in 1732.[1]

That Landon, like his four brothers, would have an

---

[1] The best published treatment of Robert "King" Carter is Louis B. Wright, *The First Gentlemen of Virginia: Intellectual Qualities of the Early Colonial Ruling Class* (San Marino, Calif., 1940; reissued Charlottesville, 1964), 248–85, but see also the short sketch in Louis Morton's excellent study of King Carter's grandson, *Robert Carter of Nomini Hall: A Virginia Tobacco Planter of the Eighteenth Century* (Williamsburg, 1941), 3–31. A contemporary estimation of King Carter's wealth is in the *Gentleman's Magazine,* II (1732), 1082.

excellent education and a generous inheritance was never open to doubt. In late 1719 or early 1720 when he was nine he went with two older brothers, Robert and Charles, to London, where he received at the private school of Solomon Low the usual classical education given to young gentlemen in England. At school he demonstrated so good a memory and such a strong inclination for learning that his father, already disposed to "make learning" an important "part of his portion," allowed him to stay on at school for four more years after his brothers had returned home in 1723. When he returned to Virginia in May 1727 at age sixteen, his father discovered him to be "a lad of good morals and of an agreeable, obligeing behaviour," "well advanced" in his education, and "very well qualified to enter upon any business." His father thought for a time of apprenticing him to a London business house "to breed him up a Virginia merchant" but eventually decided to teach him the business of plantation management so that he could follow in the footsteps of himself and his three older sons.[2] After at least a brief stay at the College of William and Mary,[3] Landon lived with his father at the family seat at Corotoman and apparently managed some of his father's Northumberland lands until 1732, when his father died. In the same year Landon, age twenty-two, married Elizabeth, daughter of the late John Wormeley, scion of another leading Virginia family, of

[2] Robert "King" Carter to William Dawkins, July 14, 1720, in Louis B. Wright, ed., *Letters of Robert Carter, 1720–1727* (San Marino, Calif., 1940), 25; same, Jan. 28, 1724, as quoted in *Virginia Magazine of History and Biography*, XXXI (1923), 39–40; to Landon Carter (hereafter L. C.), July 5, 1723, in Robert Carter Letter Book, 1723–1724, Virginia Historical Society, Richmond; to John Falconar, May 16, 1727, and Dec. 16, 1727, and to James Bradley, May 17, 1727, in Robert Carter Letter Book, 1727–1728, Alderman Library, University of Virginia, Charlottesville; Robert Carter Diary, May 25, 1727, Alderman Lib.

[3] *A Provisional List of Alumni, Grammar School Students, Members of the Faculty, Members of the Board of Visitors of the College of William and Mary in Virginia, from 1693–1888* (Richmond, 1941), 11.

Rosegill in Middlesex County across the Rappahannock from Corotoman.[4]

King Carter left Landon a bounteous legacy. Through both his wife and his brothers and sisters, Landon was as well connected as any man in the colony. His sisters had married into the Burwell, Harrison, Page, Braxton, and Fitzhugh families, and his oldest two brothers into the Hills and Churchills.[5] Moreover, his father had provided him with a sizable estate. He already owned over 15,000 acres in the western part of the Northern Neck, his share of two large grants of 41,550 and 50,212 acres made by his father in 1724 and 1730 to Landon, his younger brother George, and seven of Landon's nephews.[6] In addition, his father bequeathed to him as least eight fully equipped and operating plantations: Round Hill in King George County; Bloughpoint, Jones Place, and Old Place in Northumberland County; and Hickory Thicket, the Fork, Mangorike, and Lansdowne in Richmond County.[7] Landon chose Lansdowne for his temporary seat. Taking "an old brick building tore down in many places and at an expence of some hundreds" repairing it, he appears to have moved there sometime in late 1733 or early 1734.[8]

[4] Jack P. Greene, ed., *The Diary of Colonel Landon Carter of Sabine Hall, 1752–1776* (2 vols., Charlottesville, 1965), May 12, 1776, II, p. 1039; Walter Ray Wineman, *The Landon Carter Papers in the University of Virginia Library: A Calendar and Biographical Sketch* (Charlottesville, 1962), 47.

[5] Morton, *Robert Carter*, 21–29.

[6] William Waller Hening, ed., *The Statutes at Large: Being a Collection of All the Laws of Virginia* (13 vols.; Richmond, 1823–35), V, 300–2.

[7] Will of Robert Carter, Aug. 22, Oct. 11, 1726, Sept. 12, 1728, June 9, July 23, 1730, and inventory of Robert Carter [1732], "Carter Papers," *Va. Mag. of Hist. and Biog.*, V (1897–98), 409–28, VI (1898–99), 1–22, VII (1899–1900), 66–68.

[8] *L. C. Diary*, Aug. 9, 1777, II, p. 1123. L. C. was still living in Lancaster Co. in May 1733 but had moved to Richmond Co. by September 1734. See Indenture of lease between Edward Barradall and L. C. "of Lancaster County," May 28, 1733, Sabine Hall Collection,

For the next two decades Carter devoted himself primarily to raising a family, improving his estate, and establishing himself as one of the leading men in Richmond County. Altogether, he had seven children that survived into adulthood. Elizabeth bore him four, Robert Wormeley, Landon, John, and Elizabeth, before her early death at age twenty-seven in January 1740. His second wife, the fifteen-year-old Maria, daughter of Councilor William Byrd II of Westover, lived only a little over two years after their marriage in 1742 but bore Carter another daughter, Maria. His third wife, whom he married in 1746, was a neighborhood spinster, Elizabeth, daughter of the deceased Thomas Beale. She bore two daughters, Judith and Lucy, before she died in the mid-1750s.[9] Through his marriages Carter added to his landholdings. His first wife brought him a thousand-acre plantation, Rings Neck, on the York River in King and Queen County,[10] and his second, a tract in Charles City County. By purchase he added several pieces in Richmond County and one in Westmoreland County,[11] and with the death of his brother George in 1741 he fell heir to two lots in Williamsburg, additional land in the western part of the Northern Neck, and two plantations: Ripon Hall in York County and the Park in Stafford County.[12] At the same time he was increasing the number of his slaves and

---

Alderman Lib., and H. R. McIlwaine, ed., *Executive Journals of the Council of Colonial Virginia* (5 vols.; Richmond, 1925–45), IV, 331 (Sept. 5, 1734).

[9] Wineman, *Landon Carter Papers,* 46–48; Epitaph for Elizabeth Carter, 1740, Carter Family Papers, Folder 1, College of William and Mary Library, Williamsburg, Va.; *Tyler's Magazine,* IX (1928), 284.

[10] Surveyor's plat of "Ring's Quarter," King and Queen Co., 1729, Carter Family Papers, Folder 3.

[11] See Wineman, *Landon Carter Papers,* 9–24.

[12] Copy of will of George Carter, Jan. 2, 1741, Sabine Hall Col.; will of Robert Carter, Sept. 12, 1728, June 9, 1730, "Carter Papers," *Va. Mag. of Hist. and Biog.,* VI (1898–99), 11–17. See also *L. C. Diary,* Aug. 9, 1777, II, p. 1123.

livestock, building a mill and other outbuildings on his property, and seating his unoccupied lands in Prince William and Frederick counties.[13] By 1750 he possessed an immense, and still growing, estate, totaling over 35,000 acres in the Northern Neck alone.[14] As soon as he had the "wherewithall," he built, perhaps with the help of architect Richard Taliaferro, a dwelling house "of taste," an airy and elegant Georgian structure high on a hill that looked southward over six gardened terraces to the Rappahannock River one and a half miles below. This new family seat, which was completed sometime in the early 1740s, and the plantation surrounding it he called Sabine Hall.[15]

But Carter in the tradition of his fellow gentry did not spend all of his energies on private affairs. Like his father and his older brothers, he early assumed an important role in the public life first of his county and then of the colony. In September 1734, within a year after he had settled at Lansdowne, Lieutenant Governor William Gooch and the Virginia Council appointed him justice of the peace and member of the quorum on the Richmond County court.[16] In this position he helped to dispense

[13] See Wineman, *Landon Carter Papers*, 9–14, and petition of L. C., Feb. 2, 1736, Richmond Co. court Order Book 1732–39, X, 360 (Feb. 2, 1736), Richmond Co. Courthouse, Warsaw, Va.

[14] See L. C.'s Account of Lands to Lord Fairfax, Sept. 29, 1767, Carter Family Papers, Folder 3.

[15] An excellent description of Sabine Hall is in Thomas Tileston Waterman, *The Mansions of Virginia, 1706–1776* (Chapel Hill, 1946), 127–36, 422. Waterman suggests that the house was built by Taliaferro (*ibid.*, 103, 107). His further suggestion—and here he follows earlier historians—that Sabine Hall was built for L. C. by his father in 1730 is clearly wrong. The entry in the *L. C. Diary*, Aug. 9, 1777, II, p. 1123, shows that King Carter did not provide a dwelling house for L. C., and the letter of John Carter to L. C., Mar. 3, 1740, Sabine Hall Col., indicates that L. C. had not yet moved from Lansdowne to Sabine Hall.

[16] *Exec. Journals of Council of Col. Va.*, IV, 331 (Sept. 5, 1734); Richmond Co. court Order Book, 1732–39, X, 226 (Jan. 6, 1735), 1748–52, XII, 128 (July 4, 1748), XVIII, 23 (Aug. 4, 1777).

justice and administer the county until his death over forty-four years later. Sometime during the following decade the vestry of Lunenburg Parish elected him to the vestry, and Gooch appointed him county lieutenant in command of militia. The former post he held until his death and the latter until new militia regulations that decreased his control over the troops prompted him to resign in early 1776.[17] He also held a variety of less important positions in the county as his collegues on the bench designated him to supervise the building and repair of roads, the construction of a new courthouse, or the collection of a list of tithables.[18] Less immediately successful in securing elective office, he was rejected by the voters of Richmond County three times, in 1735, 1742, and 1748, before they finally returned him in 1752 to represent them in the House of Burgesses in Williamsburg.[19]

With his election to the Burgesses Carter's public career took a new turn. Thenceforth he operated at two levels, never neglecting his duties in Richmond County but increasingly concentrating his attention upon concerns of the colony as a whole. Immediately upon his entry into the Burgesses he became one of its most active members, and during a legislative career that stretched

[17] See Richmond Co. court Order Books, 1752–55, XIII, 22 (Mar. 5, 1753); L. C. to Lord Botetourt, Nov. 1, 1768, and to John Dixon and William Hunter, Jr., May 1776 (?), Sabine Hall Col.; and Norborne Berkeley, Baron de Botetourt, to L. C., July 31, 1769, Emmet Collection, 6197, New York Public Library, New York.

[18] See Richmond Co. court Order Books, 1732–39, X, 636 (July 4, 1738), 1748–52, XII, 194 (Aug. 7, 1749), 1756–62, 336 (May 5, 1760).

[19] Richmond Co. poll, July 21, 1735, Fairfax Papers, Brock Collection, Box 227, Henry E. Huntington Library, San Marino, Calif.; Henry R. McIlwaine and John P. Kennedy, eds., *Journals of the House of Burgesses of Virginia* (13 vols.; Richmond, 1905–15), *1742–49,* 34–35 (May 24, 1742); Richmond Co. court Order Book, 1748–52, XII, 353; Lucille Griffith, *Virginia House of Burgesses, 1750–1774* (Northport, Ala., 1963), 83–90, 222–23.

6

over sixteen years until 1768, when he finally failed of reelection because, as he put, he did not "familiarize" himself "among the People,"[20] only Speaker John Robinson, Peyton Randolph, Richard Bland, his brother Charles Carter of Cleve, and Edmund Pendleton consistently played more important parts in the counsels of the House.[21] At his first session he secured appointment to the powerful standing committees for privileges and elections and for propositions and grievances, and after 1756 he was usually chairman of the standing committee on courts of justice.[22] As a writer of some reputation he helped prepare formal addresses, and along with Richard Bland he became the public defender of the House, publishing pamphlets and newspaper essays upholding its stand on the pistole fee, paper currency, and the Two-Penny Act.[23] A strong advocate of vigorous measures against the French during the French and Indian War,[24] he also con-

---

[20] *L. C. Diary*, Apr. 1, 1776, II, pp. 1008–9.

[21] See Jack P. Greene, "Foundations of Political Power in the Virginia House of Burgesses, 1720–1776," *William and Mary Quarterly*, 3d Ser., XVI (1959), 486–506.

[22] See *Burgesses Journals, 1752–58, 1758–61, 1761–65, 1766–1769, passim*; Hening, ed., *Statutes*, VI, 454, 524, VII, 13, 76, 276, 289, 568.

[23] See Jack P. Greene, "Landon Carter and the Pistole Fee Dispute," *Wm. and Mary Qtly.*, 3d Ser., XIV (1957), 66–69, for the establishment of L. C.'s authorship of both *A Letter from a Gentleman in Virginia, to the Merchants of Great Britain, Trading to that Colony* (London, 1754) and an essay in the *Maryland Gazette* (Annapolis), Oct. 24, 1754. His authorship of *A Letter to a Gentleman in London, from Virginia* (Williamsburg, 1759), a defense of the paper currency act passed by the Virginia Assembly in 1758, is indicated by obvious similarities of style and organization to his other writings. Other evidence for his authorship of this tract is presented by John M. Hemphill, II, in *Wm. and Mary Qtly.*, 3d Ser., XV (1958), 410. L. C.'s two pamphlets on the Two-Penny Act are *A Letter to the Right Reverend Father in God, the Lord B——p of L——n* (Williamsburg, 1760) and *The Rector Detected* (Williamsburg, 1764).

[24] See L. C. to George Washington, Apr. 27–29 (?), 1756, in Stanislaus Murray Hamilton, ed., *Letters to Washington and Accompanying Papers* (5 vols.; Boston and New York, 1898–1902), I, 236, and *L. C. Diary* Aug. 22, 1754, May 14, 1755, I, pp. 111–12, 123–24.

sistently and adamantly opposed British encroachments upon American rights after 1763. He claimed the distinction of first raising the alarm against the Stamp Act in the Burgesses and of inspiring that body in the fall of 1764, six months before Patrick Henry's famous resolutions of the following May, to protest that measure in petitions to the King, Lords, and Commons.[25] Over the following decade he poured forth a steady stream of essays in support of the American cause.[26] From September 1774 through the middle of 1775 he was chairman, usually by "unanimous" election, of the series of committees that administered the county in the months after the breakdown of

[25] On this point see *L. C. Diary*, July 14, 25, 1776, February 23, 1777, II, pp. 1057, 1063, 1082–83; L. C. to George Washington, Oct. 31, 1776, in Peter Force, ed., *American Archives* (Washington, 1837–53), 5th Ser., II, 1304–07.

[26] L. C. published mainly in the *Virginia Gazettes* both under his own name and under a variety of pseudonyms, including C—R—, L—C—, B—E—, Honest Buckskin, An American, An Associating Planter, Experience, and probably others. Political pieces in the *Gazettes* that can be definitely identified as his either from manuscript drafts in the Sabine Hall Col. and Carter Family Papers or through pseudonyms known to have been used by Carter are in Alexander Purdie and John Dixon's *Va. Gaz.*, Apr. 4, Aug. 1, Oct. 17, Nov. 6, 1766, Apr. 20, July 13, 1769, Mar. 22, 1770, Oct. 3, 1771, and July 28, 1774; William Rind's *Va. Gaz.*, Sept. 1, 1768, June 1, Sept. 14, 1769, Apr. 26, June 14, Dec. 13, 1770; Nov. 11, 1773, and Apr. 7, May 12, 1774, and Purdie's *Va. Gazette*, Feb. 12, 1775, Mar. 28, 1777. Pieces in the *Md. Gaz.* are in the issues for Oct. 24, 1754, and May 8, 1766. In addition there is evidence that L. C. may have published essays in the *Maryland Journal* (Baltimore) and the *Pennsylvania Evening Post* (Philadelphia) in 1777. (See Francis Lightfoot Lee to L. C., Feb. 28, Apr. 15, 1777, Lee-Ludwell Papers, Va. Hist. Soc.) He also published at least one piece and probably more in London (*L. C. Diary*, undated 1774, II, p. 917, and Francis Lightfoot Lee to William Lee, April 6, 1770, Brock Col., Box 4). That he wrote and undoubtedly published many other essays on the debate with Britain is clear from the numerous manuscript drafts scattered in the various collections of his papers. In the Sabine Hall Col. alone there is the draft of a long pamphlet on the Stamp Act, dated Nov. 30, 1765, plus at least twelve shorter essays ranging over virtually every important issue between 1765 and 1776. There are three other pieces in the Carter Family Papers (Folders 3 and 104) and one each in the Wellford Collection in the library at Sabine Hall, Warsaw, Va., and in the Brock Col. (L. C. to Joseph Royle, June 3, 1765).

royal authority and enforced the Continental Association.[27] Though he sharply disagreed with Thomas Paine's *Common Sense,* preferring to be compelled to independence rather than to seek it actively, he continued to give wholehearted support to the American cause after the Declaration of Independence, his spirits rising and falling with the tide of American fortunes in the war.[28]

When Carter died on December 22, 1778, at the age of 69,[29] a eulogist could have pointed to the accomplishments of a full and active life. He had obviously been more than an ordinary man. A devoted and tireless public servant, he had played a significant part in every important political event in Virginia during his career in the Burgesses between 1752 and 1768 and through his writings had perhaps helped sustain the determined resistance to Britain over the succeeding decade. He was almost certainly the most prolific and most published author of his generation in Virginia and perhaps in any of the colonies south of Pennsylvania, producing at least four major pamphlets and nearly fifty essays for the *Virginia Gazettes, Maryland Gazette,* and other newspapers in both England and America. His scientific writings had won for him election to the American Philosophical Society in 1769 and to the Virginia Society for the Promotion of Useful Knowledge when it was founded in 1773.[30] All of his children had made acceptable marriages, and he had provided for them

[27] *Va. Gaz.* (Purdie), Feb. 17, May 19, June 2, 1775, (Dixon), Jan. 14, 1775; Robert Wormeley Carter Diary, Sept. 22, 1774, American Antiquarian Society, Worcester, Mass.

[28] See *L. C. Diary,* June 14, 1776, II, pp. 1049–50; L. C. to George Washington, July 30, 1777, Washington Papers, LII, 101, Library of Congress, Washington, D.C.

[29] Family Bible, Sabine Hall.

[30] *Proceedings of the American Philosophical Society, Held at Philadelphia, for Promoting Useful Knowledge* (Philadelphia, 1884), XXII (July 1835), Part III, No. 119, 19–20 (Nov. 15, 1768), 35 (Apr. 21, 1769); and *Va. Gaz.* (Rind), Apr. 14, 1774.

amply, giving large dowries to his four daughters and large estates to his three sons. Including property already transferred to his sons before his death, he left an estate consisting of nearly 50,000 acres of land, perhaps as many as 500 slaves, and a large amount of additional wealth in livestock, buildings, and personal possessions—a fortune second to few in the state.[31]

But these accomplishments could not gloss over a sense of bitter disappointment that nagged Carter throughout his final years. For some reason he had failed—and he knew he had failed—to make any lasting impression upon his generation, to achieve that recognition among his contemporaries that would assure him of a place in history. That his disappointment was well founded is attested by his subsequent obscurity, an obscurity that may on the surface seem to be deserved. Even a full biography with the traditional plea for recognition of a long-neglected figure would not raise him to that position to which he aspired and to which he liked to think he might be entitled. Neither would it add much to what is already known about the configuration of Virginia society during his lifetime. There is little in the general pattern of his life to distinguish him from any number of his contemporaries among the Virginia gentry. With some slight changes, a few minor substitutions of names, dates, places, details, his biography might be any of theirs. Yet for history to say no more about Landon Carter would do him a grave injustice. What distinguishes him from his fellows, what may yet attain for him the recognition of which he thought he had been deprived are the large body of writings he left behind and, more especially, his diary, a

[31] L. C.'s will is in *Va. Mag. of Hist. and Biog.*, XXIX (1921), 361–62. His inventory is in the Sabine Hall Col. For the property of his sons a few years after his death, see Jackson T. Main, "The One Hundred," *Wm. and Mary Qtly.* 3d Ser., XI (1954), 372. His children's marriages are described in Wineman, *Landon Carter Papers*, 47–48.

diary that served first as a simple record of day-to-day activities, then increasingly as a companion to which in the loneliness of old age he could confide his thoughts and lay bare his frustrations. For unlike similar documents of his contemporaries his diary has a reflective quality and an openness that provide, perhaps better than any other single source, a suitable vehicle for a journey into the mind of one member of Virginia's eighteenth-century plantation gentry. An analysis of the individual psychology of one or even several members of a group can probably never be an adequate substitute for the study of the social psychology of the whole group, but a probing of the basic motivations, preoccupations, aspirations, fears, and impressions of Landon Carter, an identification and explanation of his central assumptions, attitudes, beliefs, values, tastes, ideals of behavior, and ethical imperatives, may at least serve as a beginning toward a clearer understanding of the psychology of one of the most important groups in the American past.

II The Imperfection of
Every Created Being

One of the most distinctive features of the personality of Landon Carter was an intense and abiding distrust of men. Whence it derived, how deep it lay within his past, are now impossible to determine, but it was an integral part of his character by the time he began keeping a diary at age forty-one. It may have been no more than the expression of an extreme shyness that he sought to mask by bold disdain for others, but whatever its origins it manifested itself in a pronounced reserve and caution in his personal relationships, an almost total cynicism about the motives and actions of his fellow men, a profound skepticism that made it impossible for him to accept anything not confirmed by his own experience, and a constant and thorough scrutiny of his own behavior. This cluster of traits and the deeper distrust with which they were associated were intimately connected with his conception of human nature.

Until the latter part of the eighteenth century it was, of course, traditional in the western world for man to have a low opinion of himself. The imperfection of man in contrast to the perfection of the gods or God had been in turn a cornerstone of Greek, Hebrew, and Christian theology, and the innate and total depravity of man was central to most Protestant theologies as they developed in the sixteenth and seventeenth centuries. Though there were some indications of the emergence of a more genial view of man as early as the last decades of the seventeenth century, few seventeenth- or eighteenth-century men in either Europe or America seriously entertained the proposition that man was naturally good or held out the hope for human progress that was so characteristic of the nineteenth century—an era appropriately styled by A. O. Lovejoy as "the Age of Man's Good Conceit of Himself." Rather, they persisted in the conception that man was both corrupt and irrational; dominated by his passions, prejudices, vanity, and interest; and perpetually deluded in thinking himself rational.[32]

That Carter shared this view of human nature was to be expected; few men depart radically from the general intellectual milieu in which they live. But his conception of man was not merely a reflection of the views of theolo-

[32] An excellent discussion of seventeenth- and eighteenth-century conceptions of human nature is in Arthur O. Lovejoy, *Reflections on Human Nature* (Baltimore, 1961), especially 1–34.

gians or philosophers; he found it in every corner of life, in the indifference and ingratitude of his overseers, the indolence and drunkenness of his slaves, the avarice and dishonesty of British merchants, the thirst for power of the clergy.[33] Everywhere he looked he constantly saw men "intoxicated with either ambition, malice, avarice, or some of the other modes of corruption," falling into error "either through temper or interest," sacrificing truth to their own vanity, sinking ultimately into depravity.[34] It was not that men were innately evil; they were merely weak and imperfect, fallible in their understanding, confined in their vision, unhappy even in their structures. Thus constituted, they could scarcely avoid falling into corruption, and "Corruption once tasted" led directly to the grossest "species of barbarity, injustice and Plunder." Vice was simply a concomitant of human nature.[35]

Carter's analysis of himself only confirmed his judgment of man. His own greatest weakness, a constant reminder of his and man's imperfection, was an almost ungovernable temper that had already acquired for him a reputation as "a passionate man" before he was twenty-five years old.[36] The repeated and occasionally violent quarrels with his neighbors, overseers, and family—each in turn "a scandalous affair,"[37] a blatant display of his

---

[33] See *L. C. Diary,* Apr. 27, 1766, Sept. 28, 1770, Apr. 7, Sept. 11, 1771, Mar. 9, 1776, July 7, 1777, Aug. 31, 1778, I, pp. 291–92, 505, 556, II, pp. 625–26, 997–98, 1107, 1148–49; *Letter to B——p of L——n,* 55.

[34] L. C. on parliamentary taxation, n.d., Wellford Col., Sabine Hall; L. C. to Joseph Royle, June 3, 1765, Brock Col.; *Md. Gaz.,* Oct. 24, 1754.

[35] *L. C. Diary,* Apr. 13, May 28, July 26, 1776, Feb. 11, Apr. 27, 1777, II, pp. 1016, 1045, 1065–66, 1075, 1102–3; *Letter to a Gentleman in London,* 20–21; *Letter to B——p of L——n,* 6, 17; *Rector Detected,* 16; L. C. on councilors' refusal to join association, [1774–75], Sabine Hall Collection.

[36] John Randolph to L. C., Mar. 3, 1735, *Va. Mag. of Hist. and Biog.,* III (1885–96), 357. See also similar hints in William Byrd II to L. C., July 26, 1742, in Moncure D. Conway, *Barons of the Potomac and Rappahannock* (New York, 1892), 193–94.

[37] *L. C. Diary,* Sept. 5, 1775, II, pp. 937–38.

own vicious tendencies—troubled him deeply and brought him continual anguish. The recurrent outbursts between him and his eldest son, Robert Wormeley, who was, as Carter remarked, "perhaps . . . equally unhappy in temper" with himself, turned Sabine Hall during the last fifteen years of Carter's life into a scene of "eternal fretting at nothing and indeed quarrelling about as little" and drove him alternately to denounce his son as his "dayly curse" and to resolve either to "remove out of his Company or forever hold my tongue."[38] "Sorry indeed and very sorry I am," he wrote in his diary in September 1775, "ever to let anything whatever alarm me into indecencies. But the man who is of a hasty temper must be ever thinking of it if he intends to conquer it or it will forever keep him under."[39] Though he could occasionally comfort himself with the knowledge that he had gained a temporary victory over his temper, no amount of resolution and effort, of remorse or contrition, seemed to enable him to make the victory complete, and he could find consolation only in the knowledge that his weakness could be "imputed to those frailties which are incident to human nature."[40] But it was not merely his temper or his passions that he had to contend with. "I think," he wrote to George Washington in May 1776, "that in general we are too much tinctured with either the interest or the vanity which most of us acquire from our cradles. I speak as from myself; it has cost me more labour to conquer such habits than ever *Hercules* had. Such an *Augean* stable is the whole world almost!"[41] If he judged men harshly, he

[38] See, for instance, *L. C. Diary,* July 6, 1766, June 23, 1773, Feb. 15–16, 1776, I, pp. 314–15, II, pp. 763, 983–84; Robert Wormeley Carter Diary, Aug. 25, 1766, Col. of Wm. and Mary Lib.

[39] *L. C. Diary,* Sept. 20, 1775, II, p. 946.

[40] *L. C. Diary,* June 16, 1771, June 23, 1773, Feb. 11, 1777, II, pp. 577–78, 763, 1075.

[41] L. C. to Washington, May 9, 1776, in Force, ed., *Am. Archives,* 4th Ser., VI, 389–92.

also saw in them reflections of his own imperfections and tried to judge himself by the same standards. There could, after all, be no greater folly than for a man to fancy "that he does not bray."[42]

The overwhelming evidence of "the imperfection of every created being" meant simply that no man, no matter what his position or responsibilities, could be expected to overcome all his evil tendencies. If a governor turned out to be "avaricious and designing," if a clergyman displayed an insatiable thirst for power, if a king "should incline to be a despot," it was primarily because they were men. By the same token, all human institutions—the British Parliament, the Virginia Assembly, the Richmond County court—could be expected to be fallible precisely because they were composed of men. "Injustice and Oppression will always be the product of an earthly Supremacy," Carter wrote in 1776, "and I am confident however Romantic writers may be as to the morality of their heroes among men, there never was that created being either single or collected . . . who ever did or even could discharge so divine a duty with impartiality and disinterestedness. I do not say there are not, nor ever were good men," he added, "but if we consider the human machine, we are not without Perpetual opportunities, though we should discover the Spirit of man to be willing to do good . . . of Observing and indeed feeling the weakness of flesh." Clearly, man could never be any more than man.[43]

This profound conviction of man's inherent weakness colored Carter's entire personality. Knowing that no man was "incapable of Error," he preferred to rely on his own

---

[42] L. C. to Alexander Purdie, Feb. 14, 1774, Sabine Hall Col.
[43] *L. C. Diary,* Apr. 27, 1777, II, pp. 1102–3; *Md. Gaz.,* Oct. 24, 1754; *Letter to B——p of L——n,* 55; *Rector Detected,* 16; L. C. to Dixon and Hunter, May 1776 (?), Sabine Hall Col.

experience rather than "upon the possitive though not always very certain accounts" of others. Seeing "every day . . . stronger reasons for" his "great caution in this world" and convinced from "more than 50 years real Observation" that there was no genuine friendship, he chose to remain aloof even at the risk of alienating his closest associates rather than to put himself in the power of imperfect men. In choosing to be aloof, he may also have hoped to hide his own imperfections and a deep sense of guilt he felt at not being able to overcome them.[44]

III Virtue Is the Best Policy

Man's imperfections, his inability ever to be *completely* good, did not mean that he was incapable of improvement. The very knowledge of his weakness was itself the greatest spur to overcome it, and the quest for virtue and honor—the determination to bridle one's passions, to resist all temptations to corruption, to act with reason and deliberation, to avoid self-delusion, to rise above a narrow concern for one's self-interests, perhaps even to become in the eyes of one's fellowmen a praiseworthy man by whose very acts and example society might be bettered—the striving to harness man and make him serviceable to himself and to society was the most important, and the most difficult, challenge confronting mankind. But it was the determination to surmount these difficulties—to meet and to overcome the challenge—that gave nobility to man, and with Landon Carter this determination was compulsive.

[44] *L. C. Diary,* Jan. 9, Feb. 9, 1776, Aug. 1, 1777, II, pp. 967, 977, 1120; *Md. Gaz.,* Oct. 24, 1754; L. C. to 2 in the Corner, [1769–70], Sabine Hall Col.

Carter's relentless pursuit of improvement was probably the dominant feature of his personality; certainly it was the central concern of what he referred to less than two years before his death as "the whole plan of my life."[45] Reflecting back over his first sixty-five years in June 1775, he characterized himself in Alexander Purdie's *Virginia Gazette* as a "sensible Gentleman, who has lived to an extreme age, preserving an unexceptionable character, as well in his publick capacity as in his private life."[46] This strong commitment to the ideal of a virtuous and honorable life, a consuming desire both to overcome his own weaknesses and to distinguish himself among men by contributing to the happiness and safety of his family and the public, was at the root of most of his behavior. "Be convinced from a life of long experience," he warned the Virginia councilors in a public letter in late 1774, "that in all endeavours whatever, Virtue like honesty is the best Policy." Dishonesty and vice might well produce some "temporary advantage," but they also brought grave penalties: "the fatal *but*, in a good Character that could hardly be forgotten among men," a persistent gnawing "in some leizure hour of reflection" of that "living worm in man Called Consciousness."[47] But more dreadful than the loss of reputation or the pangs of a guilty conscience was the prospect that virtue once lost might never be recovered, that temptation once succumbed to might never be overcome, that, as Carter suggested in warning against submission to the Tea Act in February 1774, corruption unless it was resisted might even "in time get the better of all Virtue." That this prospect was no idle fear was repeatedly illustrated during Carter's last

[45] *L. C. Diary,* July 28, 1777, II, p. 1117.
[46] *Va. Gaz.* (Purdie), June 30, 1775.
[47] *L. C. Diary,* Mar. 1, 1774, II, pp. 798–99; L. C. on councilors' refusal to sign the Continental Association, [1774–75], Sabine Hall Col.

years—years when his entire structure of values seemed to be under assault by the combined forces of political corruption in Great Britain and social decay in Virginia—by the abandonment of his sons, Robert Wormeley and John, to gambling; the passion of his personal body servant, Nassau, for drink; the failure of his overseers to tell him the truth; the decline all around him among friends and associates of the traditional sense of public duty; the continual machinations of "departments of ill designing men" in British politics. It was only too apparent that vice, as he lamented in his diary in October 1774, was "a thing most easily learned and but seldom . . . got over."[48]

The attainment of virtue by creatures so strongly attracted to vice required enormous strength of character and unusual self-discipline, qualities Landon demanded from both himself and others. He liked to think of himself as "a *Steady* friend to Society" and admired those men who, like his son-in-law William Colston, seemed to be of a *"steady* turn of mind."[49] For weakness, whether the weakness of his "upland friend" for sacrificing a "Vast estate" to satisfy the demands of an extravagant wife or that of his grandson Landon for his "constant and extravagant" indulgence of an "outrageous" temper, he had only contempt.[50] And inconstancy and vacillation— playing "wanton with the *Wind,*" as Carter felicitously phrased it in *The Rector Detected*—were perhaps the grossest forms of weakness. He was disturbed to discover in 1752 during his first session in the House of Burgesses

---

[48] See *L. C. Diary,* Mar. 7, 1772, Sept. 23, 1773, May 2, Oct. 8, 1774, Apr. 8, 1776, Apr. 16, 1777, II, pp. 657, 778, 800, 868–69, 1013, 1091–92; *Va. Gaz.* (Rind), Sept. 1, 1768; L. C. to Purdie and Dixon, Feb. 14, 1774, Sabine Hall Col.

[49] *L. C. Diary,* July 19, 1776, II, pp. 1059–60; L. C. to Dixon and Hunter, May 1776 (?), Sabine Hall Col.

[50] *L. C. Diary,* June 16, 1771, Feb. 8, 1776, II, pp. 577–78, 977.

that his fellow politicians "should run like Bowls," and he denounced the "famous Mr. Richd. Bland" as "a Shuttle Cock and without faith" for not remaining "steady in one instance to the Opinion he set out upon this Session unless it was immediately determined."[51] Although he had no illusions about his own infallibility and repeatedly asserted his eagerness to recede from error, he was strongly convinced, as he declared in condemning the Stamp Act in the *Maryland Gazette* in 1766, that *"Right* and *Wrong"* were "so immutable in their Ideas, and so much at variance in their Natures" that it was inexcusable either to confuse one with the other or not to adhere tenaciously to an opinion one had once decided was right.[52] Refusing to sanction even the slightest sacrifice of truth, he disputed with neighbors over trifles, insisting that "truth and justice have no virtue" if they did "not shine in a farthing as well as in a million."[53] The man in quest of virtue could ill afford to give an inch, to relax for a moment, to permit even the slightest indulgence of any weakness. Although all faults could be attributed to man's natural imperfections, not attempting to overcome them reduced "Things to a *primitive State of Barbarity"* and opened the door to all vice. Any "Sharper" could say "when he is detected in cheating at a Gaming-Table, that others would do the same, had they the same Opportunity or Advantage," Carter declared in *The Rector Detected,* and "every Bunter" could "justify her Course of Life, by saying that no Woman could be chaste if she did not dread the Loss of her Reputation."[54] But every man was obliged to attempt to overcome his natural imperfections, and without a continual and steady effort he had little chance of success.

[51] *L. C. Diary,* Apr. 11, 14, 1752, I, pp. 99, 101; *Rector Detected,* 12.
[52] See *L. C. Diary,* Dec. 26, 1774, II, p. 905; *Rector Detected,* 5; *Md. Gaz.,* May 8, 1766.
[53] *L. C. Diary,* Jan. 25, 1770, Oct. 5, 1774, II, pp. 350, 865.
[54] *Rector Detected,* 23.

But strength and discipline alone were not sufficient to overcome those imperfections. Given the almost certain probability of self-deception, of incorrectly perceiving the *real* reasons for his behavior, it was necessary for man to subject his motives and deportment to a rigorous examination to make sure that "Malice" had not taken "possession of his heart" or that he had not unwittingly yielded to his passions. "Always in your Leisure hours," Carter advised the twenty-three-year-old George Washington in 1755, "regard the inward Man." Only through the kind of careful self-study recommended by this injunction could one hope to know himself well enough to subdue his baser tendencies. Even a comprehensive and persistent probing of the inner self might not produce the necessary self-knowledge. There was no more difficult task than to know one's self, and Carter was persuaded, as he wrote to a more mature Washington in May 1776, that no more "truly sublime compliment" could be paid to any man than "That he was a master of himself!"[55] This drive for self-mastery, though less pronounced in Carter than in some of his contemporaries such as John Adams, contributed to a strong tendency toward introversion, to a painful concern to discover how he was doing in his struggle with his passions in his pursuit of distinction.[56]

Perhaps the best weapon man had in the struggle for self-mastery was reason. For Landon reason was that "improvement . . . which in every body is impressed by nature," that faculty which permitted man, alone among all creatures, "to govern" his instincts, to employ, as Carter suggested in some informal comments on René Le Bossu's *Traité du poème épique*, "the knowledge and

[55] *L. C. Diary*, Feb. 6, 1776, II, p. 976; L. C. to Washington, Oct. 7, 1755, in Hamilton, ed., *Letters to Washington*, I, 108; May 9, 1776, in Force, ed., *Am. Archives*, 4th Ser., VI, 389–92.

[56] See *L. C. Diary*, June 16, 1771, June 23, 1773, Aug. 12–13, 1777, II, pp. 577–78, 762–63, 1125.

experience and hopes and fears of Effects and consequences . . . to promote or avoid . . . Causes according
as they are known or Suspected to be advantageous or
detrimental to us." That reason was continually hindered
in its operations by passions, prejudices, vanities, and
interests within man or by the constraint of tradition or
"some Superior or Ascendant Power"[57] upon him did not
have to mean, as Alexander Pope had suggested in his
Essay on Man, that man need *always* be animated by his
passions rather than his reason.[58] Indeed, Carter insisted
that every man was obliged to use his reason, however
unreliable it might be, to check his passions and to guard
against habits and tendencies, arguments and practices,
that were "Vastly against all or any spark of reason."[59]
However difficult the task might be, and he never suggested that it might be easy, it was essential for the
attainment of virtue and distinction; and he insisted that
wisdom and "real sensibility" came only to the man "who
knowing his human machine" endeavored "by his reason
to counteract it" so that he might never sacrifice "his
good sence" to his passions or permit those passions to
exceed the bounds of his reason.[60]

The ideal of moderation had traditionally been regarded as one of man's most useful devices for curbing his
passions, and Carter made it his constant concern to live
up to that ideal. He was thoroughly persuaded, as he
wrote in his diary in August 1770, that "Extremes in any

[57] *L. C. Diary,* Mar. 6, 13, 1752, Feb. 15, 1770, I, pp. 75, 84–85, 357; L.
C., "Jotting on Epick defined from Bossue," n.d., Wellford Col.; L. C. to
George Washington, May 9, 1776, in Force, ed., *Am. Archives,* 4th Ser.,
VI, 389–92.

[58] For an analysis of this aspect of Pope's thought, see Lovejoy,
Reflections on Human Nature, 42–45.

[59] *L. C. Diary,* Mar. 9, 1752, I, p. 78; *Letter from a Gentleman in
Virginia,* 13; L. C. to Old Friend, May 14, 1769, Sabine Hall Col.

[60] *L. C. Diary,* June 16, 1771, May 10, 1774, I, pp. 577–78, II, p. 809;
Letter to B——p of L——n, 3.

thing are bad."[61] Without restraint, without a strong determination to maintain the utmost prudence in one's
appetites, habits, and behavior, one could, despite his
reason, indulge himself in the rankest of his passions until
he had either suffered himself to fall prey to the "most
abandonned of all Vices" or perhaps even destroyed himself completely. The penalty for the "imprudent habits of
that kind of intemperance generally called good living"
was no less than the corruption of "the whole machine
with one kind of Morbidity or another," and the failure to
moderate one's desire for wealth and power could result
only in "a dropsical thirst" which increased the more it
was indulged.[62] Nor were the "horrid" consequences of
self-indulgence limited to one's self; a man's intemperate
actions might ruin his family or plunge his entire country,
as Carter inferred in his *Letter to the B——p of L——n*
in 1760, "into Confusion and Despair."[63] A strict adherence to the goals of moderation and prudence was essential for the man in pursuit of distinction, and Carter
sought not only to maintain "every degree of temperance"
in his own behavior but also to appear "to the whole
World as a constant Enemy to . . . *all Kinds of extravagant Life.*"[64]

One of the most pernicious forms of extravagance in
the world of Landon Carter was the pursuit of pleasure,
and his firm belief that "good living" could never be
combined successfully with the quest for distinction manifested itself in a deep antagonism to most diversions. To
be sure, he had his own pleasures: smoking his pipe,

[61] *L. C. Diary,* Aug. 14, 1770, Oct. 13, 1774, I, p. 465, II, pp. 875–76.
[62] *L. C. Diary,* Sept. 28, 1770, Apr. 19, 1771, Apr. 8, 1776, I, pp. 505
558–59, II, pp. 1012–13.
[63] *L. C. Diary,* Sept. 14, 1774, II, pp. 857–58; *Letter to B——p of
L——n,* 37.
[64] *L. C. Diary,* Sept. 11, 1770, Dec. 31, 1771, Oct. 13, 1774, I, p. 487, II,
pp. 642, 876; *Rector Detected.* 13.

riding out to view his plantations, studying and writing, maintaining a table of quality, conversing with friends and visitors about matters of moment, providing a week-long entertainment for all of his neighborhood friends each January, even having an occasional dram with other leading men of the county at the ordinary after court or militia muster.[65] But these and most other amusements he permitted himself were either useful or infrequent, and those he preferred most were useful. His reading and writing, certainly his own greatest diversions, were always purposeful. They had to provide some "Agreeable instruction," and his dictum that poetry should have "some moral truth . . . as the foundation of the Work" accurately expressed his attitude toward all forms of literature and all varieties of knowledge.[66] He had no taste for frivolity. A play to which Peyton Randolph and his older brother Charles Carter of Cleve dragged him in Williamsburg in 1752 was a surfeit of "Stupidity and nonsense delivered from the mouths of Walking Statues"; a dinner with several Essex County friends at Whitlock's Ordinary in Hobbs Hole was "time . . . very disagreeably spent among some laughing Gentlemen."[67] For Carter life was too serious for levity and the quest for distinction too difficult to waste many moments in nonpurposeful endeavors. But what he found even more disagreeable than the useless and the trivial, what he even more stoutly disdained, was the intemperate devotion that he constantly observed in his sons Robert Wormeley and John, in his grandson Landon, and in many of the younger generation of Virginians to those "bewitching" diversions—cards, dancing, liquor, horse racing, "running

---

[65] See, for instance, *L. C. Diary*, Jan. 14, Nov. 25, 1770, June 25, 1774, I, pp. 346, 527, II, p. 835.
[66] L. C., "Epick defined from Bossue," n.d., Wellford Col.
[67] *L. C. Diary*, Apr. 15, 1752, Feb. 20, 1771, I, pp. 103, 539.

about"—that not only served no useful purpose and "at best" produced no more than "some serious and Mortifying reflexion how idly, injuriously, and simply" one had spent his time, but also became ends in themselves and thereby led men away from "the more solid improvements of the mind, the Body and the estate" which could be expected to "effect something Permanent that will be injoyed hereafter."[68]

Just as Carter was opposed to all diversions that became ends in themselves and served no useful purpose, so also was he hostile to "v[ai]n shew," empty ceremony, and concern for form rather than substance. In November 1770 he offered no apologies to especially important guests, the John Randolph and Philip Ludwell Lee families, for not serving wine with dinner when he had "neither estate nor constitution to Justifie the use of it," and in September 1772 he was disturbed to see the wife of one of his plantation managers "act the part of a fine Lady in all her towering aparell with at least two maids besides her own girl to get the dinner and wait upon her," preferring instead to "have seen the diligent industrious woman." English education, he came to believe by the 1770s, epitomized all the evils and emptiness of ostentation. "The general importers of it nowadays," he recorded in his diary, "bring back only a stiff priggishness with as little good manners as possible," a concern for nothing more important than "the particular cut of a waistcoat, the multi oval trim of a hat, or the cast of a buckle," and knowledge of nothing but "the foppishness of fancy." An excessive interest in appearances, like a devotion to frivolous pleasures, could never be expected to produce anything more than "bodily and momentary injoyments" that

[68] *L. C. Diary,* June 27, 1772, Feb. 12, Sept. 14, 1774, Mar. 8–9, 1776, II, pp. 703, 795, 857–58, 996–98.

died "away with the hour generally, if they" did "not introduce some horrid conclusion."[69]

Even more alarming than the possibility that one might, by devoting himself exclusively to the pursuit of pleasure, waste his entire life away in "folly, idleness, and dissipation" was the danger that he could in time lose his freedom by becoming a slave to his passions. The man "that loveth drink," Carter declared in July 1766, "must love every thing, to get at it" and, like the man with a passion for gaming, could "so continue as to sell the part of the Community he lives in and at last sell himself" just to satisfy his lust. Carter complained in February 1774 that Robert Wormeley had become through his devotion to gaming "every man's man but his own." "No affrican is so great a slave," Carter declared the following October, as the man with a "Passion for gaming." Gaming, along with the avarice that Carter was convinced produced it, could also destroy a man's freedom by reducing him to beggary, for the man who gamed risked losing "his own Liberty" quite as much "as his fortune," and if a man lost his estate, nothing could "keep him free and independent."[70] Carter's lifelong exposure to Negro slavery provided him with a constant and vivid reminder of just how "miserable" and abject the slave was,[71] and he was persuaded that the only certain way to avoid being reduced to such a wretched condition was to take "constant care" never to be left "without the Cork Jacket of Independence." He was invulnerable, he declared in 1759, as long

---

[69] *L. C. Diary*, Mar. 23, Nov. 21, 25, 1770, Sept. 14, 1772, Sept. 14, 1774, I, pp. 372–73, 525, 527, II, pp. 728, 857–58.

[70] *L. C. Diary*, June 5, 1766, June 6, 1773, Feb. 12, Oct. 9, 1774, Mar. 9, 1776, Sept. 2, 1777, I, p. 314, II, pp. 755–56, 795, 870, 997–98, 1129.

[71] Instances of this kind of reaction to Negro slavery may be found in *L. C. Diary*, July 10, Sept. 19, 1771, II, pp. 589, 636; L. C. to Mr.——, Nov. 30, 1765, Sabine Hall Col.

as he had his "excellent little Fortress . . . built on a Rock . . . of *Independency*" for protection, and the preservation of his independence was with Carter an obsession, in many ways his most prized and most jealously guarded possession. "Independency," he wrote in 1769, was the "base or footstool on which Liberty can alone be protected," and for Carter there was absolutely no doubt that the man without liberty could never be a man of virtue.[72]

The pursuit of distinction required not only that a man maintain his independence but also that he always act with disinterestedness and impartiality. Nothing was any more destructive to virtue nor more pervasive in man than the desire for wealth and power—what in the eighteenth century was generally subsumed under the term *ambition*—and the narrow concern for selfish interests that usually attended it. Carter never ceased to be impressed by the "Predominancy of Gain among mankind," and for him no one group illustrated the evils it produced better than merchants. Mostly "Men of low and selfish Notions," they were "well vined in the sinister modes of gain," driven "by an uncommon Kind of Partiality," masters of "the arts of Speculation and deception," and "no otherwise *interested in the Country,* than in the dirty demands" they had against it. "It is . . . well known," he warned the public in September 1776 in arguing against the encouragement of mercantile enterprise in Virginia, "that the *Lex Mercatoria* indulged to any extent, must soon introduce a manifest interruption of the *Jus Commune* in any State." Trade, he declared in May 1774 in exasperation against his British creditors, "is a Profession that kicks Conscience out of doors like a fawning Puppy,"

[72] *Letter to a Gentleman in London,* 27; L. C. to Purdie and Dixon, Fall, 1769, Folder 3, Carter Family Papers; L. C. to Wm. Rind, Oct. 1773, Sabine Hall Col.

and the man who abandoned conscience, who permitted himself to be governed by "self and gain alone," could be expected to "Sacrifice . . . every duty, whether Moral or religious" to his self-interest. Any man who "makes an *Idol of his Interest,*" Carter cautioned in *The Rector Detected,* "must make a *Martyr* of his *Integrity.*"[73]

Of "all the Failings incident to human Nature," however, the most pernicious—"the worst disposition to be possessed of in the world"—was man's insatiable "thirsting after . . . Power," his "innate disposition to rule," to be the "sole determiner in all things." This "partial Fondness for Power incontroulable" appeared everywhere: in Speaker John Robinson's attempt to dominate the proceedings of the House of Burgesses; in the clergy's attempts to secure the disallowance of the Two-Penny Act, a law the Virginia legislature had considered necessary for "the Welfare of the Community"; in British merchants' acting as "lording Tyrants over their unfortunate Debtors"; in Parliament's extravagant claims to supremacy over the colonies in the Declaratory Act; in "the secret inclination of some" members of the new republican government in 1776 "to an arbitrary sway"; in the desire of Robert Wormeley to dominate life at Sabine Hall. Wherever this "Grasp" for "Power" appeared, it was certain that both public good and private virtue would be sacrificed to self-interest and partial ends.[74] The failure to check one's ambition—to subdue one's desire for wealth and power—was an open invitation to corruption. One might by dint of purely selfish ambition become

[73] *L. C. Diary,* Sept. 28, 1770, May 20, 1774, Jan. 31, 1776, Aug. 8, 1777, I, p. 505, II, pp. 813, 970, 1122; *Letter to a Gentleman in London,* 6–7, 9, 27; *Rector Detected,* 24; L. C. to Wm. Rind, Oct. 1773, and to Purdie, Feb. 14, 1774, and Sept. 1776, Sabine Hall Col.

[74] *L. C. Diary,* Mar. 13, 1752, Sept. 18, 1775, May 29, 1776, I, pp. 84–85, II, pp. 944–45, 1046; *Md. Gaz.,* Oct. 24, 1754; *Letter to a Gentleman in London,* 11; *Letter to B——p of L——n,* 55; *Va. Gaz.* (Rind), Sept. 1, 1768, (Purdie and Dixon), July 28, 1774.

wealthy and powerful and in the process acquire fame and *apparent* distinction among men. But in the very process he would necessarily have forfeited the impartiality and disinterest that were the central characteristics of *real* distinction. Carter reserved his admiration for those men who sought to "ennoble their Lives by *real* Goodness." "I only wish that every one was, as you have shown yourself to be," he wrote George Washington in May 1776, "not so much in quest of praise and emolument to yourself as of *real* good to your fellow-creatures." For himself he disdained "all Praise or Commendation" that did not arise from the true glory of genuine *"public Virtue,"* preferring that *"contented Condition"* that arose only from the knowledge that one actually was, and not only appeared to be, virtuous.[75]

This desire to *be* and not merely just to *seem* could not be fulfilled by the simple checking of one's passions, by a constant devotion to the ideals of reasonableness, moderation, independence, and disinterestedness; it required positive accomplishments for the benefit of one's family and country, accomplishments that came only through hard work. Throughout his life Carter seems to have adhered closely to his father's injunction to him as a lad of thirteen studying at Low's School in London to be "a good Boy and mind your Book" and to "Improve your time Suitable to the charge I am at upon you."[76] Believing that "a constant diligence" not only would "effect great matters" but also would check the natural human tendency toward "degenerating into indolence" and prevent man from falling "into a disponding way" and making "even the common cares of life a very heavy weight upon

[75] *Letter to a Gentleman in London,* 12; *Letter to B——p of L——n,* 40; *Rector Detected,* 33; L. C. to Washington, May 9, 1776, in Force, ed., *Am. Archives,* 4th Ser., VI, 389–92.
[76] King Carter to L. C., July 5, 1723, Robert Carter Letter Book, 1723–24, Va. Hist. Soc.

himself," he demanded hard work and a careful use of time both from himself and from everyone around him.[77] At court it was he who always acted as the "Spur" to the other justices, resorting to cajolery, threats, and a continual "calling out" to secure some "order and dispatch of Publick business," to rouse his fellows out of "their laziness" and "spirit" them "up to a diligent discharge of their duty to the public."[78] On his plantations he held his overseers and slaves to a rigorous schedule. He prided himself on never getting a day behind in his plantation work, and he always planted the fullest crop possible, persuaded that those who planted short crops expecting to produce larger yields by more thorough working only accelerated the natural human tendency to degenerate "into indolence when there is not a visible necessity to be otherwise." On the same theory he always sought to keep his slaves busy, believing that there was "nothing so certain as spoiling your slaves by allowing them but little to do; so sure are they from thence to learn to do nothing at All." He reluctantly permitted the use of mechanical implements, for he was convinced that "Carts and plows only serve to make Overseers and people extremely lazy." "It is a certain truth," he wrote in his diary in April 1770, "that wherever they are in great abundance there is the least plantation work done . . . for both Overseers and Negroes imagine this or that work will be quickly done with the plows and Carts and of course are very little solicitous to do their proper parts of the business."[79] Nor did he demand any more work from others than he did

[77] *L. C. Diary,* Feb. 28, Apr. 30, Sept. 11, 1771, I, pp. 544, 566, II, pp. 625–26.

[78] *L. C. Diary,* May 9, 1770, Apr. 14, 1772, Mar. 1, 1774, I, p. 405, II, pp. 668–69, 799.

[79] *L. C. Diary,* Apr. 12, Aug. 14, 1770, Sept. 11, 1771, May 27, 1772 June 25, 1774, May 12, 1776, I, pp. 386–87, 465–66, II, pp. 625–26, 694–95, 834, 1038–39.

from himself. His careful and in many cases direct supervision of his plantation work and his painstaking diligence in recording his agricultural successes and failures in his diary so that he "might correct . . . his . . . errors" leave no doubt that he held himself to the same high standards of industry.[80]

For the man of distinction learning was as important as hard work; it served both as a means to acquaint oneself with the past mistakes and successes—the accumulated knowledge—of man and as a base for adding to that knowledge. "It is the business of man," Carter wrote in his diary in February 1771, "to find out causes where he can in order to prevent any evil that may attend," and much of his adult life seems to have been devoted to that end. His early success at Low's School, the considerable amount of erudition sprinkled through his enormous literary output, the copious annotations in the margins of his large collection of books at Sabine Hall, his "particular Respect" for "Men of Learning," his attempt to establish a free school in Richmond County, his extreme sensitivity about his intellectual achievements, his presumption in the midst of the War for Independence in asking Washington for a map of the fighting area to gratify his "geographical genius," his attribution of the chronic "Vertiginous disorder" of his later years to his "too great a desire for knowledge, an intense reading and observing upon all things," the diary itself—all testify both to his learning and to a passionate devotion to the pursuit of knowledge which probably exceeded that of most of his contemporaries among the Virginia gentry. This devotion derived not only from his desire to excel but also from his usual reserve and introversion and from the sheer pleasure he received from reading and writing. In his diary for April

[80] *L. C. Diary*, May 29, 1772, II, p. 697.

1777 he remarked that before the deterioration of his eyes he had never been less alone than when by himself— *"Nunquam minus Solus, quam cum solus"*—and he probably always felt more comfortable at home among his books than he did in company. Nor did this tendency decrease as he grew older, for the "desire to read" became, especially during the last decade of his life, the chief antidote to the loneliness of old age.[81]

A man who was convinced of the imperfection of every man could also be expected to believe in the imperfection of every author, and Carter was a thoroughly skeptical reader. He was willing to accept "the possitive though not always very certain accounts of the learned," as he wrote during a controversy over the transit of Venus in 1769 and 1770, only when they did not contradict his experience. Although he thought that theory was necessary to explain practice, he was at heart a complete empiricist and always insisted on the primacy of experience over theory. The very "Imperfectness of theory," he told Dr. Walter Jones in May 1772 in defending the great Leiden physician Hermann Boerhaave against Jones's teacher, Dr. William Cullen of Edinburgh, meant that there was always "room for experience to improve it"; and he was persuaded, he wrote in his diary in July 1775, that "reasoning on General Principles . . . is cursed nonsense in every Science whatever, for General Principles are like General rules, subject to multitudes of Exceptions and perhaps no two instances can happen but must differ from those Principles according to Attending Circumstances."[82]

[81] *L. C. Diary,* Feb. 24, 1771, Aug. 18, Sept. 2, 22, 1772, Feb. 24, 1776, Apr. 13, 1777, I, p. 540, II, pp. 713, 720, 731, 987, 1090; *Rector Detected,* 24; L. C., "Proposals for establishing a free school in Richmond County," n.d., Sabine Hall Col.; L. C. to Washington, Nov. 2, 1776, in Force, ed., *Am. Archives,* 5th Ser., III, 482.

[82] *L. C. Diary,* Mar. 17, 1771, May 26, 1772, July 22, 1775, Feb. 6, 1776, I, p. 548, II, pp. 692–93, 926, 976; L. C. to 2 in the Corner, [1769–1770], Sabine Hall Col.

To know anything, then, required a thorough and precise knowledge of all its complexities, all its subtleties.

The same obsession with thoroughness that caused him to plow his land deeper and to work his fields oftener and more systematically than anyone else and the same concern for accuracy that made him keep exact records of business transactions and a detailed diary manifested themselves in his own writings in tediousness and verbosity. Anyone who reads his pamphlets and essays will recognize the probable justice of Thomas Jefferson's charge that Carter's "speeches, like his writings were dull, vapid, verbose, egoistical, smooth as the lullaby of the nurse, and commanding, like that, the repose only of the hearer." Though Carter undoubtedly could and did, as he said on one occasion, mouth "as Caesar till I shook the Senate" and awaken even Jefferson, he always preferred, as he wrote in his *Letter to a Gentleman in London* in 1759, to rely upon the "evident Truth" of his argument rather than any "extraordinary Eloquence" to persuade his readers and hearers. He could not write shorter essays, he declared in his piece on the weevil fly published in the American Philosophical Society *Transactions*, because they would be "less clear and intelligible." The lack of specific information was perhaps the most serious failing in a writer. "It is amongst the oddities in Authors, whether travellers, Essayists, or Naturalists," he complained in July 1775, that "they all write as if every reader knew beforehand what they were writing of as well as themselves; for this reason in hardly any one instance do they give any Particulars." Without "Particulars" their writings were not fully useful to the reader. Completeness and exactness were the ways to truth, and Carter in his preoccupation with truth and his suspicion of form always made a point, as he declared in *The Rector Detected,* of penning his arguments "with such Precision and Plainness . . . that every Reader, the least acquainted with the Subject I have written upon, might understand them."[83]

Carter's desire to push back the boundaries of knowledge was symptomatic of the greater obligation he felt to serve the public; devoted public service was the hallmark of the man of virtue, the characteristic that distinguished the man of real quality from the man who was merely in search of fame, wealth, and power. Carter thought both that man "was at first created" for the performance of "social duties" and that the responsibility for those duties fell squarely upon "the polite and more considerate part" of society, that group which had the time, resources, and virtue to care for the concerns of the public expertly and impartially. It was to the upper classes that a country looked "for Prudent advice and assistance," for "Patterns or examples," and there was nothing more "commendable" than "to let men see our good works that they may take example by them in their conduct to each other and to the happiness and safety of their Country."[84] This concept of upper-class leadership carried with it a heavy burden of responsibility, and Carter was one member of the Virginia gentry who shouldered that burden eagerly and with the same high seriousness with which he accepted his obligation to lead a virtuous life. He repeatedly sought to use his learning for the benefit of the public,

[83] *L. C. Diary,* Apr. 20, 1752, May 25, 29, 1772, Oct. 5, 1774, July 27, 1775, I, p. 107, II, pp. 692, 697, 865, 930; Stan V. Henkels, ed., "Jefferson's Recollections of Patrick Henry," *Pennsylvania Magazine of History and Biography,* XXXIV (1910), 406; *Letter to a Gentleman in London,* 28; *Rector Detected,* 3–4; L. C., "Observations concerning the fly weevil, that destroys wheat," *Transactions of the American Philosophical Society,* Old Ser., I (1771), 217; L. C. to My Friend, [1774?], Sabine Hall Col.

[84] *L. C. Diary,* Nov. 6, 1771, Oct. 6, 1774, Sept. 11, 1775, Feb. 23, 1777, II, pp. 638, 866–67, 941, 1084; Hening, ed., *Statutes,* VII, 289, 568; L. C. to Purdie and Dixon, Fall 1769, Carter Family Papers, Folder 3; L. C. to Wm. Rind, Aug. 1772, Sabine Hall Col.

publishing the results of his scientific and agricultural experiments in the *Gazettes,* using his skill in medicine to minister to his "whole neighbourhood," advising friends and acquaintances about the law, supporting measures to encourage arts and manufactures in the colony.[85]

Carter's most conspicuous public service was in the political realm. As a justice of the peace he continually endeavored to improve the quality and the efficiency of the administration of the county. In January 1735 at the second meeting after his appointment to the court he sought to remedy certain deficiencies by securing an order empowering him "to send to England for what law books he shall think necessary for Richmond County" and "to acquire a table of weights and measures according to colony law." For the rest of his life he was constantly trying to secure some "order and dispatch of Publick business" and to preserve "order an [d] decency . . . in the Co[unty]." The same devotion to duty that caused him to worry about "the possibility of a wrong Judgement . . . either through temper or interest" also drove him to leave a sick bed to attend court so that he might not contribute to the delay of the administration of justice. Even after independence, when he felt that the ingratitude of many people in the county had given him ample

---

[85] *L. C. Diary,* Sept. 11, 1771, Sept. 14, 1775, II, pp. 625–26, 942–43. Known or highly probable writings on agricultural and scientific subjects by Carter are in *Trans. Am. Phil. Soc.,* Old Ser., I (1771), 218–24, on the fly weevil; in the *Va. Gaz.* (Rind), Sept. 14, 1769, on a hurricane, July 26, 1770, on the transit of Venus, Nov. 19, 1772, on the fly weevil, and on Apr. 14, 1774, on the care of lightning victims; *Va. Gaz.* (Purdie and Dixon), Aug. 30, Sept. 13, 20, Oct. 4, Dec. 13, 1770, Jan. 31, 1771, on the transit of Venus, and Dec. 3, 1772, on the prevention of the plague; *Md. Gaz.,* Dec. 21, 1758, Apr. 5, 1759, on the corn moth, Mar. 10, 1763, on lucern. Manuscript pieces by Carter include letters to Purdie and Dixon, Oct. 1, 1770, on the transit of Venus, Carter Family Papers, Folder 3, to 2 in the Corner, 1770, on the transit of Venus, in the Sabine Hall Col., as well as undated essays on the body fluids and the cultivation of hops in the Sabine Hall Col.

cause to withdraw from the court, he could not, despite strong resolutions to the contrary, "desert" his "Duty to" his "Country," and when a "worthy member begged" him to "come to give weight and order to the Proceedings," he resumed his place on the bench, convinced from the observations of a long life that "order and comfort arises from the appearance only of some good man." Nor was he any less devoted to his duties as a burgess. To be a burgess was an "honour" in itself, but just to have the post was not enough for Carter; only by being "a *diligent*" and, he might have added, unusually active "Member of the assembly" could he think himself "truely meritorious." In seventeen years of service, he declared in 1774, he had missed the meeting of the House only when he was sick or when he wished to protect himself "in the small Pox time." The same "true Sense of the Duty he" owed "to his Country" drove him to take up his pen to defend the Burgesses and the colony in each of the long series of controversies that preceded the outbreak of the War for Independence. His greatest satisfaction seems to have been the knowledge that he had done his duty to his community, and the role he delighted in most was, as he signed himself in a letter to Alexander Purdie's *Virginia Gazette* in September 1776, as the public's "most devoted and Assiduous Servant in all my endeavours for their real good."[86]

Even with the strictest adherence to this elaborate structure of values, the most intense devotion to self-discipline, self-mastery, reason, moderation, improve-

---

[86] Richmond Co. court Order Books, X, 1732–39, 230 (Jan. 7, 1735); *L. C. Diary*, Apr. 6, 1772, Mar. 1, 1774, Feb. 15, Aug. 8, 1777, II, pp. 668, 799, 1076–77, 1121; *Letter from a Gentleman in Virginia*, 3–5; *Rector Detected*, 3–4; L. C. to Joseph Royle, June 3, 1765, Brock Col., Huntington Lib.; L. C. to Wm. Rind, Oct. 1773, to My Friend, (1774?), to Dixon and Hunter, July 1776, and to Purdie, Sept. 1776, Sabine Hall Col.

ment, independence, disinterestedness, hard work, learning, and public service, Carter knew from repeated experience that no man could achieve true distinction or measurable success in his earthly enterprises without the help and favor of God. No seventeenth-century New England Puritan was any more deeply impressed with the omnipotence of God and the ultimate dependence of man upon God's will than Landon Carter. He was not, as he admitted to George Washington in October 1776, "enthusiastically religious" in the conventional sense. He was a devout Anglican who took his duties as vestryman in Lunenburg Parish seriously, but his bitter attacks on the clergy during the controversy over the Two-Penny Act and his repeated embroilments with local ministers William Kay and Isaac Giberne were indicative of his antagonism to and suspicion of the clergy. Although he believed strongly in a close connection between church and state so that the religious power might remedy "the Imperfections of the Civil," he favored toleration and was opposed to burdening non-Anglicans with the support of the established church. Nor does he seem to have had much interest in formal theology, preferring instead the "Practical godliness" so strongly recommended to him by his father.[87] Though he had little use for many of the trappings of religion, he was an intensely religious man. His piety permeates the diary. He was continually thanking God for his blessings, asking forgiveness for his sins, seeking divine favor in his endeavors. He could not help

---

[87] *L. C. Diary*, Mar. 10, 1752, Aug. 19, 1771, June 4, 1774, I, p. 81, II, pp. 616–17, 819–21; Carter to Washington, Oct. 21, 1776, in Force, ed., *Am. Archives*, 5th Ser., II, 1304–7; *Letter to B——p of L——n*, 4, 7, 14–16, 24; King Carter to William Dawkins, July 14, 1720, in Wright, ed., *Letters of Robert Carter*, 25; William Kay to Bishop of London, June 14, 1752, in William S. Perry, ed., *Papers relating to the History of the Church in Virginia, 1650–1776* (Hartford, 1870), 389–91.

worrying that he might have "imperfectly conceived" God's commands or that he might "have possibly deserved" any "inconveniency" that befell him. His religion was his chief comfort in the face of adversity and failure, his source of inspiration whenever he fell into a "disponding way," and when during his last ten years a "multitude of infirmities" brought him severe pain and the resulting confrontation with the certainty of death even "Produced a long dream of entertaining many dead People" and made each symptom seem like "a harbinger of death," his religion gave him hope and helped him keep up the "Cheerful" appearance that, as he noted in October 1774, he believed was his "only insincerity."[88]

Religion also served Carter as a handmaiden in his quest for distinction. Though he had no doubt that God was supreme and that man was completely at His mercy, he liked to believe that God was also just and favored the man who helped himself, who used his "skill, care, and diligence" as fully as he might and who sought to live by His word as closely as an imperfect being might. By doing his best to live a virtuous life and obey God's commands, however, a man could control his destiny only up to a point; in the last analysis it was God's will that would be done, and a man could do no more than use "his best endeavour" and "trust in his God." "In all things," Carter wrote in his diary in February 1772, "I do the best I can and relye on Superiour mercy for the success of my endeavours." When God did not reward his efforts, a man could only accept his misfortune with resignation and humility, knowing that no human was "too great to brook

[88] *L. C. Diary,* Aug. 14, 18, 1770, Feb. 27–28, Apr. 29, July 15, Aug. 18, 1771, May 16, July 2, Aug. 18, 1772, June 23, 1773, Oct. 1, 9, 1774, Sept. 11, 16, 1775, Feb. 15, 1776, Aug. 12–13, 1777, Aug. 18, 21, 1778, I, pp. 465, 468–69, 543–44, 565, II, pp. 591–93, 615, 684, 704, 713, 763, 860, 870, 940–41, 943, 988, 1125–26, 1145–46.

37

misfortunes" at the hand of God, that, as Carter prayed in July 1771, "if God favors, all will be well. And if he should not what sensible Mortal could think of Existing a moment."[89]

However God might finally choose to reward or punish his efforts, Carter never for a moment ceased trying to do everything in his power to make himself worthy of any favors God might wish to bestow upon him, and the quest for virtue and distinction meant more to him than even love or friendship. Neither his affection for his immediate family nor the fatherly attachment he felt toward some of his overseers ever prevented him from trying to hold them to a strict adherence to the same rigid code by which he lived. Though he had genuine compassion and a deep sense of responsibility for his slaves, he never hesitated to use the whip or any other punishment "not barbarous"—even to frightening Toney the carpenter into work by having him "make his own Coffin to be laid up in and buried"—to keep them to their duty. Keeping Negroes busy was especially important, not only because they might meditate their freedom or their "master's destruction" if they had too much idle time, but also because they were less honest and more imperfect than white men. Unlike other men, who were "spurred on to diligence by rewards," "kindness to a Negroe" seemed to be "the surest way to spoil him," and only by maintaining strict discipline could the master fulfill his responsibility to the slaves to keep them from lapsing into a life of dishonesty and vice. "Indeed, Slaves are devils," Carter declared in disgust in August 1778, "and to make them otherwise than slaves will be to set devils free." He was one Virginia planter who had no inclination to permit his Negroes, as

[89] *L. C. Diary*, Aug. 2, 22, Sept. 19, 1770, July 15, Aug. 13, 1771, Feb. 11, May 8, Aug. 7, Sept. 24, Oct. 14, 1772, Feb. 28, 1777, I, pp. 459–60, 472, 493–94, II, pp. 591–93, 611, 653, 677, 710, 733, 740, 828, 1088.

he sarcastically commented in July 1776, to "glut" their "genius for liberty which" they were "not born to."[90]

Carter held his friends and associates outside his family to the same standards. He insisted both that every "Proper individual" was "obliged to Judge" for "the benefit of the Community" and that all men should be judged by merit and not by friendship. In his conviction that candidness was the best policy and that for men "to be so much on the guard, as to be always concealed" was "contemptible," he never tried to hide his disapproval. The result was that he was never a popular man. Indeed, some responded to him with intense dislike and perhaps even actual hate. William Jordan, a Richmond County freeholder, vowed in 1742 that he "would give a Hogshead, or a Hundred Gallons of Rum, rather than Mr. Carter . . . should go Burgess; and that he never should go Burgess." To his indentured secretary, Owen Griffith, Carter was a "Boisterous Tyrant"; and someone else bitterly satirized him in two long poems in Purdie and Dixon's *Virginia Gazette* in 1767. Carter's trouble was that he demanded perfection from men knowing that they, like himself, would always be imperfect, and his "stern behavior" and apparent cynicism offended people and made them uncomfortable. "How might he be revered," an anonymous and friendly critic suggested in verse in November 1768 just before Carter's constituents turned him out of the Burgesses, "Would he strive rather to be loved than feared." "Let him relax," he added, "and we are all his own." But relax was the very thing Carter could never do.

[90] *L. C. Diary*, Apr. 27, May 4, 1766, June 28, Aug. 14, 21, Sept. 28, 1770, July 10, Sept. 17, 19, 1771, May 27, 1772, June 14, 1774, July 13, 1776, Apr. 20, 1777, Aug. 31, 1778, I, pp. 292, 295, 429–30, 465–66, 471, 505, II, pp. 589, 632–33, 635–36, 694–95, 827, 1056, 1095–96, 1148–49; *Rector Detected*, 25; L. C. to Dixon and Hunter, May 1776 (?), Sabine Hall Col.; epitaph on Elizabeth Carter, 1740, Carter Family Papers, Folder 1.

His vigil over himself was constant, and if he was critical of the weaknesses of others, it was because he was intimately acquainted with his own imperfections. He never demanded anything from others that he did not ask of himself, and he was persuaded that no man was more honest or more "Patriotic" than "the man who owns he had split upon a rock, and . . . points it Out to others, that they may avoid it." If others objected to his judgments, it was because they either failed to consider them impartially and with "good sense" or deliberately sacrificed truth and justice for friendship. For Landon Carter either alternative was impossible. He could never, as he replied to his anonymous critic, permit justice to "pine, or Right give up its whole/To purchase love, so painful to the Soul." For the man in quest of honor and virtue neither love nor friendship nor applause was worth the forfeiture of integrity.[91]

IV   A Noble Struggle

Landon Carter seems to have been irresistibly drawn to politics. For forty-four years from 1734 until his death in 1778 he was actively involved in the political life of the colony, and his keen sense of public responsibility, his conviction that devoted public service was the most important mark of the man of distinction, his tendency to immerse himself in any question or problem he encountered, his penchant for thorough and systematic analysis,

[91] *L. C. Diary,* Mar. 14, 1770, Mar. 9, 15, 31, 1776, I, p. 368, II, pp. 997, 1001-2, 1007-8; *Letter to B——p of L——n,* 35; *Va. Gaz.* (Purdie and Dixon), June 11, Aug. 13, 1767; *Burgesses Journals, 1742-49,* 34-35 (May 24, 1742); "Verses before Election" and Carter's reply, Nov. 1, 1768, and Owen Griffith to L. C., Dec. 21, 1771, Sabine Hall Col.

and his compulsion to write all of his observations down that they might be of some service either to himself or to the public—all of these characteristics combined to produce a body of formal and informal political comment that exceeds in quantity that of any other Virginian of his generation and probably reveals more fully than the writings of any other individual the framework of political assumptions and ideas within which his generation of Virginians operated. To what extent those ideas derived from his reading and his early experience in the relatively stable political environment of Richmond County and Virginia in the years before 1754 is now impossible to say, but they were certainly amplified and enlarged, if not in many cases fully articulated for the first time, in response to the dramatic events of subsequent decades: the French and Indian War; the pistole fee, paper money, and Two-Penny Act controversies; the pre-Revolutionary debate with Britain; war and independence. They grew out of and were dependent upon his conception of human nature, and they represented in general an attempt to apply to the public realm those values and standards of behavior around which and on which he thought all men should build their private lives. Just as the greatest challenge to man as an individual was to protect himself from his own evil tendencies, so the principal end of government was to protect men from each other, and the central question behind most of Carter's political inquiries was how a government necessarily composed of imperfect men could ever fulfill that end. That this was the basic dilemma of man in society became increasingly manifest with each new succession of events between 1754 and 1778, and its apparent insolubility only made the search for a solution the more compelling. Indeed, man's persistence in the search even in the face of almost certain failure was perhaps, as Carter suggested in mid-1776, his most "noble Struggle."[92]

Carter's notions about politics rested upon two assumptions about the nature of man: first, that he was a social being drawn naturally and inevitably into associations with other men and, second, that he was an imperfect creature who, if left entirely to his own devices, could not be expected to act for the good of society as a whole. Few men could see beyond their own narrow horizons or could rise above "the general proneness in Mankind, to favour their own Errors." But much more dangerous than this natural weakness was the conscious malevolence of "men of a depraved Turn." They invariably sought to "shake off every Restraint," and their passion for fame or money or power was so great that "even halters about" their necks could scarcely prevent "them from broaching the most destructive measures" to society. To promote happiness and order by securing the life, liberty, and property of every individual from the arbitrary rule of such men, to seek to operate upon the principles of freedom and justice rather than oppression and injustice, and to disappoint "every *avaritious, merciless* Man, in his Desires of preying upon the Necessities of the People" were, then, the primary functions of government.[93]

For a government to fulfill these functions it was absolutely necessary, Carter was convinced, that it always attend to the general "Good of the Community" rather than to the particular needs of any individual or group within the community. It was upon this principle that

[92] L. C. to Dixon and Hunter, May 1776 (?), Sabine Hall Col.

[93] *L. C. Diary*, Feb. 24, 1776, II, pp. 986–87; L. C. on taxation, n.d., Wellford Col.; L. C., to Botetourt, Nov. 1, 1768, to Purdie, Feb. 14, 1774, and Sept. 1776, to Dixon and Hunter, May 1776 (?), Sabine Hall Col.; L. C. to Washington, Oct. 21, 1776, in Force, ed., *Am. Archives*, 5th Ser., II, 1304–7; *Letter from a Gentleman in Virginia*, 3–5, 16, 33–35; *Md. Gaz.*, Oct. 24, 1754; *Letter to a Gentleman in London*, 25; *Letter to B——p of L——n*, 5, 17, 43, 59; *Va. Gaz.* (Rind), Apr. 4, 1766.

Carter built his defense of the Two-Penny Act against the attacks of the clergy and the Bishop of London in 1760. That law, he argued in his *Letter to the B——p of L——n,* "was a Thing absolutely necessary to be done" for the welfare of the colony and was "therefore just in itself." To oppose it because it injured a small group within the colony, as the clergy had done, was to demonstrate a willingness "to pave the Way to egregious Extortion on a whole Community" to benefit "but a very few Individuals," and it was a "great Absurdity," he argued, to suppose "that a Part is greater than its Whole; or, in other Words, that some Individuals ought to be considered, even to the Destruction of the Community, which they compose." That doctrine, he declared, was "worthy of those alone who are confined within the narrow Circle of private Profit, and have no Relish for *publick Good,* that interferes with their dirty Schemes of Gain." Later in the controversy he used the same argument in *The Rector Detected* against the Crown's right to disallow laws colonial legislatures had thought necessary for the good of the colonies. "For let the Prerogative be carried to what Height it will," he contended, "it cannot, without great Injustice, be construed to the Destruction of the Prince's Virtue; which I shall not stick to define to be that Goodness which inclines him . . . to acquiesce at all Times in the Agreement of his Subjects amongst themselves, in any Part of his Dominions, when that Agreement does not affect his own *royal Right* in any *sensible* Manner, or the Rest of his Subjects of his Kingdom in any Manner *whatever.*" Even the royal prerogative had always to give way before the public good. Almost immediately after the outbreak of the War for Independence in early 1775 Carter declared in his diary that he thought the welfare of the community justified the suppression and perhaps even the expulsion and punishment of any "Traytors in opinion to

43

their Country." Anyone not choosing to join the Continental Association or refusing to take an oath of allegiance to his country was, as he declared in February 1777, certainly "an enimy to his Country." Rejecting the argument that "Tories . . . only differed in Opinion" and that that difference might somehow be "for the good of the Country," he contended that to permit a part of the community to differ in opinion from the majority when the very being of that community was at stake "might be destructive of the whole." "One or a few" could never "be better Judges of" the public "Good than was the multitude," and if that good required the suspension of "Private Justice" or the suppression of the individual liberty of the minority that opposed it, then it was, as in the case of the Two-Penny Act, "a Thing absolutely necessary to be done" and "therefore just in itself."[94]

The "Good of the Community" demanded not only that its corporate interests always be preferred to those of any part of it but also that no group within it—and especially no group with political power—ever be granted any special privileges. Such a grant might appear initially to be for the welfare of the public and might even operate in a salutary way so long as those to whom it was made were "undebauched by corruption." But given the "frail nature" of man and especially his "innate disposition" to seek power over his fellow creatures, no individual or group of men, however virtuous or deserving they might seem, could be trusted not to turn such privileges to their own private advantage and to use them to establish a despotism or "a mere Aristocratic power." In Carter's eyes aristocracy, which he defined as the rule of a small group for their own private ends, was "an Arbitrary and an Oppressive" form of government.[95] This belief that no

[94] *Letter to a Gentleman in London,* 20–21; *Letter to B——p of L——n,* 5, 19, 29, 50–51, 55; *Rector Detected,* 23, 30.
[95] *L. C. Diary,* July 29–30, 1775, Feb. 20, 1777, II, pp. 931–33, 1078–79; *Letter to B——p of L——n,* 19.

men could be trusted with too much power led Carter to advocate rotation in office after independence and to oppose attempts by any group to secure special privileges. Thus in August 1772 he attacked the ruling of the Virginia Council that a councilor could be tried only in the General Court in Williamsburg or in the court of the county in which he lived. To make such an "extraordinary distinction . . . between a councellor and a Commoner," he charged, carried "an Aristocratical Complexion"; and he warned that "such a vast extension of power . . . united in one set of men" might introduce great "inconveniency to the Community." Even if the councilors who made the ruling managed to resist the temptation to seek still greater privileges and more power, they might be replaced by "men of great extravagance, always dextrous in the slavery which they generally introduce to support themselves," and then, Carter cautioned, "poor Denmark let thy unhappy history apply the fatal conclusion." "No Judicious Constitution" could ever "give the least countenance" to such a "partial privilege." One of the "most essential" tasks of government, Carter had declared in *The Rector Detected* back in 1764, was "the Preservation of the greater Number of Individuals against an almost certain Oppression from the lesser Number," and the only certain way to prevent the lesser number from gaining the ascendancy was to preserve the absolute legal equality of all subjects. In attacking the Council's ruling, Carter emphasized the obligation assumed by the justice of the peace in his oath "to *do equal right to the poor and to the rich, after their cunning, wit, and power according to law.*" That obligation underlined the greater responsibility of a government to make sure that no group was ever accorded any special status, privilege, exemption, or benefit. "Subjects have no Pretence, one more than another," he declared in 1759 in his *Letter to a Gentleman in London;* "they must all equally enjoy an Advantage, or suffer a Calamity whenever it attends a Community." Such an equality was the best guarantee against the emergence of an authority within the state that could not be controlled by the public.[96]

But if a good government avoided giving any advantages to or placing too much power in the hands of the rulers or any other special group, it also had to be careful not to place too much influence in the hands of the people in general, and Carter was as opposed to "popularity"—by which he seems to have meant both the tendency for men with political ambitions to seek office by catering to the whims of the people and the demand of the voters that their representatives act in direct accordance with their sentiments—as he was to aristocracy. As early as October 1754 he argued in a debate with the "favourers of Popularity" over the nature of representation in the House of Burgesses that in all cases except those that "related particularly to the interest of the Constituents alone" a representative should "be Governed" not by the collective "sentiments of his Constituents" but by "his own Reason and Conscience." Obviously, a man who permitted himself to be closely bound by his constituents could not act with that spirit of disinterestedness and impartiality that Carter thought necessary for every public servant, and he was deeply suspicious of the motives of any man who permitted himself to be so bound. It was clear to Carter that such a man would promise anything to the freeholders and even practice the most "rascally deceit" to "suit" his "ambitious schemes" to be "chosen a representative only to carve a good plan for himself." Such a hypocrite, once in office, could be ex-

---

[96] *L. C. Diary,* May 9, 1774, May 29, 1776, II, pp. 808, 1046; *Letter to a Gentleman in London,* 10; *Rector Detected,* 22; L. C. to William Rind, Aug. 1772, and to Dixon and Hunter, May 1776 (?), Sabine Hall Col.; Francis Lightfoot Lee to L. C., Nov. 9, 1776, Emmet Col.

pected to serve not the public but himself either by conspiring with men of similar hue to establish "an Aristocratic Power" or by selling himself to his country's enemies, forgetting "poor Liberty" in the process and delivering the country "into slavery." Carter had no doubt, as he wrote to George Washington in October 1776, that "popularity" was as real an "enemy to freedom" as the most corrupt ministers in Great Britain. Nor was it worth while for a man of virtue to play the game in the hope of eventually bringing the people back to their senses. Though his son Robert Wormeley "kissed the arses of the people and very servilely accommodated himself to" them, they "shamefully" and ungratefully threw him out of office at "a kind of April fool" election on April 1, 1776, after seven years of faithful service. "But it is the nature of Popularity," Carter cynically wrote in his diary after the election; "She I long ago discovered to be an adulteress of the first order; for at any time let her be most sacredly wedded to one man she will even be grogged by her gallant over his shoulder."[97]

Perhaps the least desirable feature of popularity was its direct effect upon the people. By early 1776, as a result of the forces set in motion by the breakdown of royal authority and the American opposition to Britain, they had become so "Poisoned" by popularity and had fallen into such disorder that they preferred to rely for their defense upon "the incontroulable will of every individual humble" rather than submit to the direction even of "the greatest and most devoted constitutional Patriot that has for ages appeared." This rejection of qualified and disinterested leaders, coupled with the tendency, also produced

---

[97] *L. C. Diary*, Oct. 17, 1754, Mar. 28–29, Apr. 1, 4, 1776, Feb. 4, Apr. 27, 1777, I, pp. 116–17, II, pp. 1006–10, 1073, 1102–3; *Rector Detected*, 8; L. C. to Washington, Oct. 21, 1776, in Force, ed., *Am. Archives*, 5th Ser., II, 1304–7.

by popularity, for each individual to pursue his own private interest "Neck or nothing" in the attempt to get ahead, led to the total neglect of public concerns. In short, as Carter lamented in March 1776, "the Public is . . . neglected . . . as the People may be concerned."[98]

Because the people in general could not be trusted to care for the interests of the public or the community, government had to depend for leadership upon the patriot, and the patriot had to have those qualities Carter invariably claimed for himself in his public writings: virtue, honor, a sense of justice, impartiality, disinterestedness, independence. In every public action he had to be moved, as Carter claimed to be during the pistole fee controversy, by no "Interest less than that of a whole Country"; he had to be, like Carter thought George Washington was, "resolved never to forget" the "citizen in the . . . rulers." He could not be attached to any party, because parties, Carter thought in common with most of his contemporaries, were the instruments of partial and interested men whose commitments to factional and private ends invariably prevented them from considering the public interest objectively and impartially. Every "good man," Carter contended in urging the Virginia councilors to join the Continental Association, "ought to act under all appointments relative to the Public."[99]

Even patriots, however, could not always be trusted to act in the best interests of the public. John Robinson, speaker of the House of Burgesses and treasurer of Virginia from 1738 to 1766, was a case in point. A man of

[98] *L. C. Diary,* Mar. 29, Apr. 9, 1776, Aug. 8, 1777, Aug. 5, 1778, II, pp. 1006, 1015, 1121, 1141; L. C. to Dixon and Hunter, May 1776 (?), Sabine Hall Col.

[99] *L. C. Diary,* Mar. 21, Apr. 11, 1752, I, pp. 89, 98–99; *Letter from a Gentleman in Virginia,* 3–5, 35; *Letter to B——p of L——n,* 10; *Md. Gaz.,* Oct. 24, 1754; L. C. to Washington, May 9, 1776, in Force, ed., *Am. Archives,* 4th Ser. VI, 389–92; L. C. on councilors' refusal to join association [1774–75], Sabine Hall Col.

great charity, benevolent intentions, "amiable dignity," and "many brilliant virtues," Robinson, Carter noted upon his entry into the Burgesses in 1752, frequently used the influence of his position to push measures through the House that Carter thought were unwise. Though he complained about Robinson's willingness to use his "weight" to overcome "reason" and disapproved of any man's having such a stranglehold upon the House, he was not especially alarmed, because Robinson seemed to be entirely without any "vitious Principles." The revelation at Robinson's death in 1766 that he had, apparently solely out of charity, loaned large sums of public money to his friends showed just how dangerous the concentration of so much power in the hands of even an honest man could be. That Robinson's actions had "proceeded from nothing fraudulent in the Gentleman, but from the humane disposition [of] charity" did not make them, at least in Carter's eyes, any less "condemnable" nor any less harmful to the public. The lesson in this incident was clear: neither the firmest patriot nor the most virtuous man could be trusted with "uncontroulable Power."[100]

Both because "Man left to his own Will over his Fellow Creatures" could, as Carter observed in his *Letter to a Gentleman in London* in 1759, "sometimes fall into such Depravations of Mind, as to become more cruel than the most Savage Beast of Prey" and because even those men who overcame their vicious nature could by falling victim to their many inperfections inadvertently injure their fellows, all men—both rulers and ruled—had to be restrained. If it were closely connected with the "civil Power" and "Civil Society," a "Religion that deters from Evil, and encourages good Actions" could, Carter thought, help remedy their imperfections, but in the last

[100] *L. C. Diary*, Mar. 13, 1752, May 23, 1776, I, pp. 84–85, II, pp. 1042–43; *Va. Gaz.* (Purdie and Dixon), Aug. 1, 1766.

analysis reliance had to be placed primarily upon law, statutory law to minister to the general welfare of the community by establishing and maintaining an "Equitable and Just" relationship among men and fundamental law—the constitution—to guarantee to the governed those basic rights that would insure that they would never be subjected to "the voluntary Mercy" of any individual or exposed to the unlimited power of an "uncontroulable" government. The fallibility "of human Understanding, as to Causes, Effects, and Consequences," Carter repeatedly argued against all attempts to limit the lawmaking power of the Virginia Burgesses, inevitably meant that statutory law had continually to be revised and altered as necessity, reason, and justice required; but the constitution, though it might sometimes have to "be aided, extended or qualified . . . to support and preserve the Community," had to be kept "as sacred as possible." As the guarantor of man's basic rights and as the instrument by which he hoped to balance harmful elements against each other—e.g., in the manner of the "Pure British Constitution" to check the tendencies toward aristocracy and popularity by mixing them together in such a way as to keep them in a constant state of equilibrium so that man might be preserved from man, that men could live under a government of impartial laws rather than of partial men—the constitution was, at least for Carter, man's most precious possession.[101]

This strong attachment to the constitution and to constitutionalism was at the heart of Carter's intense opposition to British policy after 1764. In each successive crisis

---

[101] *L. C. Diary*, Mar. 6, 1752, I, p. 75; *Letter from a Gentleman in Virginia*, 11–12, 19, 22–23, 29; *Md. Gaz.*, Oct. 24, 1754; *Letter to a Gentleman in London*, 14–15, 19–21; *Letter to B——p of L——n*, 5–7, 15–16, 19, 46, 50–51, 53, 55; L. C. on taxation, n.d., Wellford Col.; L. C. to William Rind, Aug. 1772, and to Dixon and Hunter, May 1776 (?), Sabine Hall Col.; L. C. to George Washington, May 9, Oct. 21, 1776, in Force, ed., *Am. Archives*, 4th Ser., VI, 389–92, 5th Ser., II, 1304–7.

from the first announcement of the Stamp Act until independence he cast himself in the role, as he wrote in September 1768, of an American "greatly struggling in the cause of liberty, to save" the "constitution from being overturned." The issue, as Carter saw it, was clear: by attempting to tax the colonies "out of the constitutional road" Parliament had threatened to destroy *"the fundamental laws of the Constitution,"* and Americans by insisting upon their "Privilege of being solely governed and taxed by Laws made with the Consent of the Majority of their own Representatives, according to the *Englishman's* inherent Birthright" were simply striving to preserve those laws and protect the "purity of the . . . constitution." To Carter the most "essential" element in that constitution was the people's right of representation, their right "freely" to "enjoy and occupy their own Properties, by being Governed and Taxed only by such laws as" their representatives agreed to. Because that right was "inherent by Birth in every *Englishman,*" those Englishmen who had migrated to the colonies had brought it with them, and the Crown, finding it "impossible for the Subject when he emigrated, to enjoy such a Right . . . in a *British* Parliament," had established "either by *Charters* or *Instructions*" the "several Legislative constitutions in the Colonies," not "as a grant of new Rights," but as "a confirmation of the people's original Right of Government." Americans, then, exercised their right of representation, not through Parliament to which they neither did nor could send representatives, but through their own representative assemblies. Thus, Carter insisted, well in advance of most other American writers who were content at the time of the Stamp Act to deny Parliament's right to tax the colonies, that Parliament could neither tax nor legislate for the internal affairs of the colonies. From the Stamp Act on, he wrote to Richard Henry Lee in 1775, he had never made any distinction between "the right of giving money and the right of making laws." Through either taxation or legislation "without representation" a man might be deprived of his liberty and property without his consent, and for that reason, as he declared in arguing against the Stamp Act, men had to be exempt "from the force of *any* Law, made without the consideration of their Representatives."[102]

That no group of Englishmen should be *"governed and taxed"* by any body or any group over which they had no control derived, of course, out of Carter's general belief that there could be no uncontrollable power in any justly constituted state. "Wherever there is a superiority in Power (considered either literally or figuratively)," he declared in 1765 while attacking the notion that Parliament had unlimited authority over the empire, "Justice seldom prevails" and "Might" usually "overcomes Right," but he warned against confusing the *"Right of exercising"* with *"the power of effecting . . . such measures."* Parliament undoubtedly could command the strength to force the colonies to submit to its authority, but such an "extravagant" exercise of power could never be justified by the constitution. Carter already conceived of the empire as a series of distinct political entities united with Britain only through the Crown, and in such a political organization it was clear that no one part of the realm could have any greater privileges or any more power than any other part, just as no well-ordered government could permit any group or individual within it to have any greater advantages or immunities than the rest of the public. There had to be an "equality of constitutional rights . . . in the whole realm"; colonists had to be

---

[102] *L. C. Diary;* May 29, 1776, II, p. 1046; L. C. to Mr. ——, Nov. 30, 1765, and to R. H. Lee, Feb. 25, 1775, Sabine Hall Col.; *Md. Gaz.,* May 8, 1766, *Va. Gaz.* (Rind), Sept. 1, 1768.

equal to Britons, and colonial legislatures, Carter strongly inferred, had to be equal to Parliament. "From my earliest acquaintance with the legislative body of my Country," Carter wrote, "I have looked upon them as an assembly, inheriting every liberty that could appertain to Britons, or the Sons of Britons." He rejected out of hand any suggestion that the Virginia House of Burgesses was "a poor epitomé of British greatness" with *"only a Corporation Right to make Bye-Laws, subject to every whimsical Alteration of some pretended supreme Legislature."* So long as the "KING OF THE WHOLE REALM" exercised that "actual Supremacy . . . in every Legislation" which "the Constitution" had provided for in giving him authority to call and dissolve parliaments in and veto laws from "any Part of the Realm," there was no "Necessity . . . for a further supremacy" in Parliament. In any case, however, such a supremacy would invariably be unjust and unconstitutional, not only because it would introduce a basic inequality of rights between Britons and Americans by setting up a power over the Americans that they would be unable to control, but also because it violated *"that Fundamental"* of the *"Constitution"*—the liberty of "every Englishman" not to be governed and taxed "by any law that has not had the actual consideration of his Representatives."[103]

The Stamp Act crisis produced in Carter, as in many other Americans, a deep suspicion that corruption had taken hold in Britain and that out of that corruption had emerged a sinister conspiracy "to reduce the subjects of Great Britain" to "slavery . . . though beginning only by degrees with those in America," and each subsequent

[103] *Letter to a Gentleman in London,* 10; *Letter to B——p of L——n,* 44; L. C. to Joseph Royle, June 3, 1765, Fairfax Papers, III, Brock Col.; L. C. to Mr. ——, Nov. 30, 1765, Sabine Hall Col.; *Md. Gaz.,* May 8, 1766; *Va. Gaz.* (Rind), Apr. 4, 1766.

stroke at American freedom over the next decade only convinced Carter of the justice of that suspicion. The Declaratory Act of 1766 was "the bill of might"—a wanton and unjustified assertion of authority conceived only to pave the way for the "base purposes" of ministerial conspirators. Unable to believe that George III himself had any "design to oppress us," Carter could only conclude during the long dispute over the Townshend Acts that "departments of ill designing men" had blocked the channel to the throne and were deliberately and vilely misrepresenting "American intentions" to further their "enslaving schemes of tyranny and oppression." The circular letter of Secretary of State Lord Hillsborough ordering the "rescinding, erasing, &c." of "resolutions in favour of liberty, made by the several Assemblies in the colonies" against the Townshend Acts seemed to be calculated to blot "out all traces to posterity, should they unhappily be born under slavery, that their ancestors did every thing that their weak situation could admit of, to support and maintain their rights to freedom." Britain, Carter was persuaded by May 1769, had sunk into a "universal state of dissipation," and he warned against any compromise that would leave the constitutional issue in any doubt, not only because he believed strongly that there could never "be any half way between Slavery and freedom," but also because it would permit "the perpetrators of such an unhappy circumstance" to "draw the curtain of Respect over the destructiveness of their intentions" so that they might bring them forth again "under the banners of a planned Corruption" when the public had relaxed its guard.[104]

The mounting evidence of the internal corruption of Great Britain and of a ministerial plot against American

[104] *L. C. Diary*, May 29, 1770, I, p. 418; *Va. Gaz.* (Rind), Sept. 1, 1768; L. C. to Old Friend, May 14, 1769, Sabine Hall Col.

and British liberty was perhaps the most important factor in Carter's estrangement from the mother country. In 1760 he could declare with complete sincerity that "Loyalty is the very Genius of the Country," and even as late as 1765 he could report with probable accuracy in one of his essays against the Stamp Act that the "Colonies . . . glory in their connection with" Britain. But Carter also pointed out in 1765 that the most valuable and unique feature of that connection was Britain's historic preservation of "the Religion and Liberties of the people" of the colonies "in their full enjoyment," and, though he adamantly denied that Americans had any intention of seeking independence, as various British politicians had charged, he did warn in September 1768 that "the desire of independency" might be the eventual result, as it had frequently been throughout history, "of impatience in suffering" over an extended period of time.[105]

The repeal of the bulk of the Townshend duties in 1770 and the period of quiet that followed, at least in Virginia, did not allay Carter's suspicions, especially because he had begun to be convinced that the same corruption that had gripped Great Britain was gaining ground in Virginia. "Pride and Luxury," he observed as early as 1754, "always find an Entrance in with Riches," and he thought that the steady rise in wealth in Virginia over the previous century was by the 1760s undermining the old "Principles of order and society," the old standards of virtue and industry, and substituting in their place dissipation, "extravagance and folly." The whole society seemed to be in decline: parents neglected to discipline their children, and children in turn neglected their "duty to Parents"; "Ladies" had "grown too delicate to look

---

[105] *Letter to a Gentleman in London,* 25; *Letter to B——p of L——n,* 38; *Va. Gaz.* (Rind), Sept. 1, 1768; L. C. to Mr. ——, Nov. 30, 1765, Sabine Hall Col.

into family affairs," and Carter himself had grown too "delicate in taste"; the younger generation, even those like Robert Wormeley who had been "well educated," had forsaken reading and learning for pleasure and "loungings," and the resulting loss of intellectual vitality had produced "a sameness in action, speech, reasoning, and expression that you would think every body only learnt from one another." Worst of all, Carter noted a sharp decline among the gentry in their devotion to public service so that "the Public duty" hardly seemed "to be anybody's concern" and few thought that there was "any kind of duty or trust in the offices they undertake." Members of the Richmond County court showed not "the least inclination even to incomode the least private concern for the sake of the public," and the burgesses, as Carter observed in April 1772, sat up "regaling or gaming till 12 every night, and rise very late, mostly unprepared and in the morning very unfit for business, by which means designing men carry on scandelous and injurious laws that take up much time, which unless they had been thrown out would ruin the Country." "Thus does Social Virtue gradually die away," he lamented, "and al[ways] some imperious obstinacy succee[d]."[106]

For a time after he became governor of Virginia in 1768 Norborne Berkeley, Baron de Botetourt, seemed as if he might be able both to frustrate the sinister schemes of the ministry and to rescue Virginians from their own corruption. "Pitcht upon to be the Agent of a dirty tyrranic Ministry," Botetourt "resisted such an employment and . . . became the instrument of a dawning happiness." "Through his active and exemplary virtue," Carter

[106] *L. C. Diary,* Mar. 23, May 9, 1770, Mar. 28, 1771, Apr. 14, Oct. 3, 25, 1772, June 29, 1773, May 12, 1776, I, pp. 372–73, 405, 553, II, pp. 668–69, 736, 744, 765, 1038–39; *Letter from a Gentleman in Virginia,* 28–29; Carter to Purdie and Dixon, Fall 1769, Carter Family Papers, Folder 3.

thought, "order everywhere revived out of that confusion that our own dissipative indolence had thrown us into." But Botetourt's death in the fall of 1770, Carter feared, would both enable "those devils" in the ministry again to inaugurate their attempts "to distress this Colony" and permit "corruption" once more to "begin the great work of enslaving this Country and in it all America." "And when we get into the way of corruption," Carter despaired, "he will [be] the cleverest man that gets the most by it. Clients will turn bribers; and the transition from the sale of private justice to that of Public liberty will [be] but easy and short." Carter liked to think that Americans might "be better situated as to avoiding of such a corruption," but he knew from experience and observation that "human nature, in America," differed "not in its frailties from the same unhappiness in other lands." Experience had also taught him that only a strict adherence to tested values could avoid such a corruption in any man and in any society.[107]

That the men in power in Britain had deserted those values became increasingly clear in the crucial years after 1773. The Tea Act of that year left Carter with no doubt that his earlier suspicions had been correct. "Nothing seems more rational," he wrote in February 1774, "than to conclude that those noble Parliament leaders, presuming on the Peaceable disposition of the Americans during those years [following the partial repeal of the Townshend duties in 1770] have ventured by a combination with the East India Company to attempt to fix this duty upon America, as a Precedent for some other Purpose as yet concealed." That purpose was revealed as the crisis deepened. By the summer of 1774 Carter could no longer escape the conclusion that George III was "one grand

[107] *L. C. Diary*, Oct. 15, 20, 1770, I, pp. 512, 516; *Va. Gaz.* (Rind), Apr. 26, 1770.

Corupter of mankind, who has from his first exertion of his disposition only shewn that he wants to establish this Slavery nearer home, by supplying himself with a new fund for Corruption" so that he might buy the people by giving them pensions and places supported, ironically, "with their own money." "Pensions and Places in Government," he angrily charged after learning of Parliament's passage of the Coercive Acts to punish Boston for the Tea Party, "are like Opiates and other various forms, not administered to remove, but to stupify some painful sensation of a disorder, till a spotted despotism like the [inevitable] Mortification concludes the dreadful scene." A "designing favourite"—a Lord North, a Lord Mansfield or any one of the other "monsters of Corruption" who assisted the King in his base enterprises—was, Carter wrote, "an occult Cancer in a State that secretly pervades about till every spring is enervated out of its Constitutional tone."[108]

To combat such corruption obviously required strong and determined action, and Carter, never much given to compromise, was now ready to go to any extreme to root it out and destroy it. Just as he had argued during the Stamp Act crisis for a more limited definition of Parliamentary authority than any other American leader, with the possible exception of his fellow Virginian Richard Bland, and had stubbornly resisted during the agitation over the Townshend duties a movement by Virginia politicians Edmund Pendleton and Robert Carter Nicholas "for meeting the Parliament half" after it had only partially repealed the duties, so in 1774 and 1775 he recommended the most drastic measures possible, convinced from the history of Britain itself that it was far better to "run into mere civil war, regardless of every thing" than

---

[108] L. C. to Purdie, Feb. 14, July 18, 1774, and to ——, [1774 or 1775], Sabine Hall Col.

"suffer . . . a precedent" against liberty "to gain the least [ground]." The Boston Tea Party, for instance, was precisely the kind of remedy the situation called for. For the Bostonians to have used tea "with the Parliamentary duty laid upon it" would by establishing "a Precedent for the fleecing . . . of" their "Properties" have cost them no less than their "whole Liberty." "There can be no Liberty without some Property not subject to be taken away from us every moment," Carter contended. Such a precedent had to "be for ever lookt upon" to be "as deadly as the most infected bale of goods"; and like all infected commodities, the tea by virtue of the *"Lex Prima Natura"—"The Law of Self Preservation"*—had to be destroyed. When some of the Virginia burgesses formed an association in May 1774 not to import any East India Company goods Carter resolved to "be hearty in it," and he insisted both in conversation with people in the county and in letters to newspapers that Americans should "have as little Commerce with" the people of Great Britain "as Possible; and farther to refuse to do them the service to determine their suits for debts since they had consented to a Manifest Violation of our whole Constitution." Only by some dramatic action of this type, he argued, could they be brought to protest "this Arbitrary Proceeding of their Parliament." By the summer of 1774 he was advocating resistance to the death if it became necessary. "I am resolved to be free or cease to exist," he wrote to Alexander Purdie in July, "I meane not by my own hand but by the hand of those who are to take my liberty from me; for one thing I certainly feel that if I am not to be free life must be a burden to me, and that he who is to take my liberty from me must be an equal enimy to my life."[109]

[109] *L. C. Diary,* May 29, 1770, June 3, 8, Aug. 8, 1774, I, p. 418, II, pp. 817–19, 821–22, 847; L. C. to Purdie, Feb. 14, July 18, 1774, Sabine Hall Col.; L. C. on taxation, n.d., Wellford Col.

As it gradually became clear during the summer and fall of 1774, first by the appointment of General Thomas Gage as governor of Massachusetts and then by his military preparations, that the British government was willing to resort to armed force to secure American compliance with the Coercive Acts, Carter seems to have become more and more alienated from both the British government and the British people. However distressing to a loyal and devoted Englishman might be the conclusion that "our mother country" suddenly had to be called "our enemies," it could no longer easily be avoided. That "natural Affection"—the most "noble base to build upon in every human System of Politicks"—which had preserved among the colonists "for near 200 years a joyous content, wrapt up in a cordial and filial respect," now seemed to have given way to complete indifference; and "indifference carried too far," Carter wrote in his diary in December 1774, "often becomes a cornerstone to hatred." Though Carter's own hatred was not yet strong enough to alienate him completely from Britain, he was arguing by October 1774 that "the duty to a Prince was cancelled by the duty to one's country," and the country he referred to was quite obviously not Great Britain but Virginia and not just Virginia as Virginia but as a part of "British America (as the Colonies are called)." Moreover, the obvious willingness of the British to use force caused him to advocate meeting force with force. "Drawn swords in the hands of freedom," he observed during the winter of 1774–75, could have truly "wonderful effects," and after Lord Dunmore, then royal governor of Virginia, had stealthily removed the powder from the public magazine in Williamsburg on April 20, 1775, Carter urged that force be used to recover it. Resisting force with force, he declared, "is the first law of nature, and such an one, that even despotism should never even fancy it can dismay."

With Gage's attack upon Lexington and Concord on April 19 and Dunmore's subsequent burning of warehouses on Virginia rivers and his attempts to create a general slave uprising by promising freedom to those slaves who would flee to his banner, Carter became convinced that the British would stop at no *"inhumanity"* or *"barbarity"* even to "Murder . . . of the aged and tender infants" and the spilling of "the blood of innocents" to "subdue America" and he thought anything was justifiable to "put to flight those British Butchers." That the British might in the end be too strong for the Americans did not matter. It was far better, he wrote in his diary in July 1775, "not to deserve this Slavery by resisting it than tamely to submit to it." Besides, he had complete faith, as he reiterated until his death in 1778, that God would favor the Americans "not from any Peculiar goodness in us, but in the cause we are engaged in." The British government had both "violated" the "rights of Nature" and sought by an "Ungrateful stretch of Power" to introduce "the most hateful of iniquities, a Tyrannic despotism in the King who rules In Great Britain with mony, and would Govern America with an iron Sceptre." "Unless the devil" were "more Powerful than the God of Justice," British corruption, if not American virtue or strength of arms, would insure American success.[110]

Carter's ardor for the American cause seems never to have weakened, but he did not think independence the best way to prosecute that cause, and from the moment he first read Thomas Paine's open advocacy of independence

[110] *L. C. Diary,* Aug. 8, Oct. 29, Dec. 24, 1774, July 30, Sept. 20, 1775, Apr. 4, 23, July 16, 1776, II, pp. 847, 890–91, 901, 932–33, 945–46, 1011, 1023–24, 1058; L. C. to Purdie, July 18, 1774, Sept. 1776; to the Independent Company of Volunteers of Richmond County, Apr. 28, 1775; to Dear Sir, Apr. and May, 1775; and to——, [1774–1775], and L. C.'s note on strife, 1775, Sabine Hall Col.; L. C. to Washington, Oct. 21, 1776, in Force, ed., *Am. Archives,* 5th Ser., II, 1304–7.

in *Common Sense* in February 1776 until independence was actually declared by Virginia the following May he argued vigorously against it. His opposition was not simple. From the beginning of the dispute he had denied that there was any foundation to the British charge that Americans were aiming at independence, writing as late as May 1775 that "we are averse to all foreign connections and only wish . . . (the navigation act submitted to)" to "be restored to an harmonious reconciliation." Always contemptuous of inconstancy and always reluctant to change his mind or go back on his word, Carter wanted to keep the dispute on the original issue, "constitutional freedom," and he did not want to put the "original justice" of "the American cause" in question, to have it in "the least sullied," by switching goals in the middle of the conflict. "What an Opprobrium must this be to the Gentlemen of the Congress, who not only denied their tendency to independency when they were charged with it by writers," he scolded in March 1776, "but have over and over again told the whole British World that they only desired to be reinstated as they were in 1763." Such insincerity placed Americans only slightly above the British. Also apprehensive lest any aid received from foreign powers as a result of independence come with strings attached that would be "equally injurious" to American liberty, he was especially concerned because everyone who favored independence seemed also to favor a republican form of government and to "declare against the English constitution, as a form of Government which freedom cannot exist under from its arbitrary tendency." "A great Stickler for that Authority," Carter could not stand to see "the Pure British Constitution . . . so reprobated" and insisted that there was as much of an arbitrary tendency in a "Republican form" as in a limited monarchy. Even after independence had become a reality and he could no

longer profitably oppose it, he chose to think that he had
been compelled to it by British tyranny "rather than to
ever have it out of choice, because," he insisted, "as a
constitution of government none was so good as the British, and though we need not be under the control of its
now depraved arbitrariness, yet it would be best for us to
embrace the same mixed form."[111]

Carter's fear of independence and republicanism and
his commitment to a "mixed form" of government derived, of course, from his longstanding conviction that a
"mixed form" was the best instrument for balancing the
several interests in society against one another and for
neutralizing the passions of individual men; both his fear
and this commitment were intensified, however, by his
observation that the tendencies in Virginia toward moral
decay and corruption that he had noted over the previous
decades seemed to have been increased rather than less-
ened by the pressures of the revolutionary agitation. "The
Representatives of the people," he noted during the agitation over the Tea Act in May 1774, seemed to "go out of
their way of their duty instead of into it." "Such is the
nature of Public Virtue in this Colony where there is such
a Cry for Liberty," he complained, "there is hardly a man
to be met with who pays the least regard to it." Even in
early 1776 with Dunmore's forces threatening the river-
sides the Richmond County Committee of Safety and the
officers of the regiment stationed at Richmond County
courthouse seemed to be more interested in gaming than
in protecting the county. "It is a melancholly thing to

[111] *L. C. Diary,* Feb. 14, 24, Mar. 28, May 23, June 14, 1776, II, pp.
980–81, 986–87, 1006, 1042–43, 1049–50; L. C. to Purdie and Dixon, Fall
1769, Carter Family Papers, Folder 3; L. C. to Purdie, July 18, 1774, and
to Dear Sir, Apr. and May 1775, Sabine Hall Col.; L. C. to George
Washington, May 9, 1776, in Force, ed., *Am. Archives,* 4th Ser., VI,
389–92; L. C.'s endorsement on R. H. Lee to L. C., June 2, 1776, in
James C. Ballagh, ed., *The Letters of Richard Henry Lee* (2 vols.; New
York, 1912), I, 200.

think of," Carter declared, "but [at] a time when [t]here is the greatest occasion for sensibility and thoughtfulness, we see nothing but folly, idleness and dissipation." He was appalled in April 1776 when even his own family objected to his grandson and "courageous Name-Sake['s]" responding to the call to duty and going off with a band of "memorable Young heroes" to repel Bartlett Goodrich, Dunmore's Tory lieutenant. "For God's sake," he protested, "what is Patriotism, if it is only to lie in a chamber, and provide against no danger, and run no Risks?" He was sure that George III "would be Glad of such Subjects in America." To Carter, the disinterested patriot and public servant who always sought to put the interests of the whole community first, this lack of spirited patriotism, the apparent discord in the face of such a "Prodigeous cause for Unanimity," and a perpetual display of selfishness that seemed to indicate that each individual was more interested in having "his own estate secured" than in saving his country meant that Virginia must indeed have gotten "into the way of corruption," and such a development boded only ill for the future of Virginia.[112]

To Carter there appeared to be a close connection between this decline of public spirit with its attendant "internal Contentions" and the "republican form we all seem to be hurrying into." That segment of society usually referred to by Carter as "commoners" had, he reported in May 1776, come to expect that "Independency" would "be a form of Government that, by being independent of the rich men, every man would then be able to do as he pleased," and the various manifestations of such sentiments in Richmond County left him convinced that they would result in nothing but "Confusion."

[112] *L. C. Diary*, May 2, 1774, Feb. 9, Mar. 9, 13, 15–16, Apr. 23–24, 1776, II, pp. 800, 977, 997–98, 1000–1004, 1023–26.

On April 1, 1776, at the election of delegates to the convention that declared independence and adopted a new constitution for Virginia, the voters of the county turned out their old representatives, Robert Wormeley Carter and Francis Lightfoot Lee, for Hudson Muse and Charles McCarty—the one, in Landon Carter's estimation, "a worthless, though impudent, fellow" and the other "a most silly though goodnatured fool"—purely, Carter suspected, with the expectation that the new representatives would vote for "an intire independence in which no Gentleman should have the least share." As if to confirm those suspicions a "certain G. R. when asked" a month later "to lend his fire lock to go against" a British tender in the Rappahannock River "asked the People if they were such fools to go to protect the Gentlemen's houses on the river side" and announced that "he thought it would be better if they were burnt down." Carter could only interpret such behavior as manifesting a desire to exclude the gentlemen—the men not only of wealth but also of virtue, learning, experience, and distinction—from their traditional exercise of political leadership. He was fearful that without some independent and disinterested gentlemen in the government demagogues would manipulate the commoners for their own selfish interests and perhaps even establish "an Aristocratic Power" that would result in a tyranny as objectionable as the British. "My only dread has been on account of this separation which" Great Britain, "her King, her ministry and her Parliament have barbarously driven us into," he wrote in his diary in late May 1776, lest "from the secret inclination of some to an arbitrary sway themselves we might fall into a worse situation from internal oppression and commotions than might have been obtained by a serious as well as cautious reconciliation." "Certainly," he continued, "it behooves him who admires Peace, order, and moderation in Government to be cautious of such People, for it is morally certain that there are such, and without the utmost timely care they will work themselves into the Hydra of Power."[113]

To prevent such a development Carter thought that "some good form of Government" had to be devised as soon as independence was declared. He did not agree with John Adams' suggestion in his *Thoughts on Government* that remedies to the "many evils that" might "possibly attend his proposal" to establish new constitutions might be left "to times of more tranquility." Adams had drawn a parallel between "corporeal and political bodies," suggesting that time and nature would "be as active in the operations of the latter as she generally is in the former." But Carter did not think the analogy a valid one. He agreed that in the corporeal body "a tranquil waiting" for "the effects of nature" would "most probably" remove the cause of a disease. But the "body politick," he argued, had to contend, not with a beneficent nature that could be counted on for assistance, but with "a second" human "nature, vicious in all its distinctions." To insure that men would not yield to that nature, would not succumb to "the common temptations of the natural passions," it was absolutely necessary, as he wrote George Washington in May 1776, to "prevent such evils in the very beginning, or never expect to do it at all," and the best way to do so was to adopt a constitution which would establish the same "mixed form" of government as the British. No other form, Carter believed, could sufficiently check the various elements in society against one another in such a

[113] *L. C. Diary,* Mar. 28–29, Apr. 1, 9, May 1, 29, 1776, II, pp. 1006–9, 1015, 1030–31, 1046; L. C. to George Washington, May 9, 1776, in Force, ed., *Am. Archives,* 4th Ser., VI, 389–92, and July 30, 1777, Washington Papers, LII, 101.

way as to insure that the government would always operate for the benefit of the entire society.[114]

In the situation of mid-1776 Carter was especially concerned that the tendencies toward popularity be counterbalanced by the forces of disinterestedness and impartiality. He did not want to have "to trust an ignorant representative to do what he pleases under a notion of leaving his constituents independent." "Do we not see that as social beings, we must necessarily be dependent on one another," he wrote in a public letter to the convention probably in May 1776, and that unless "every individual in this state of freedom has an equal Capacity in the several essential parts of it by which we are to preserve this (not unfitly Stiled) bark of freedom" there is a "necessity of reposing every here and there in the State, a limited as well as an accountable, though not a confined power, that the sails, rigging, tar, and halon of the Vessel may be all skilfully as well as properly Conducted." A well-run ship of state had to have a strong power—limited, of course, by the constitution—placed in the hands of those men of more than common capacity, those men with sufficient learning and public spirit to navigate it properly; and such a power, Carter argued, would in no way be "a restriction on freedom," for "without some such thing," he believed, "freedom must destroy by its own confusion." "No Authority need be"—and he might have added ever ought to be—"uncontroulable. But certainly the controul ought not to lodge with those only who are to be governed by it."[115]

Making a constitution, then, was a momentous enter-

[114] L. C. to George Washington, May 9, 1776, in Force, ed., *Am. Archives,* 4th Ser., VI, 389–92.
[115] L. C. to Dixon and Hunter, May 1776 (?), Sabine Hall Col.; L. C. to George Washington, May 9, 1776, in Force, ed., *Am. Archives,* 4th Ser., VI, 389–92.

prise that could at best be only partly successful. No matter how well the job was done, "Injustice and Oppression" would "always be the product of an earthly supremacy" because it would always be in the hands of imperfect men. Yet Carter was persuaded that with the proper mixing of various interests it was possible for imperfect men to construct a workable, if not in all respects completely satisfactory, political instrument. But they could only do so, he felt, by eschewing popularity, recognizing that all members of society were dependent upon one another, and making sure that political leadership was entrusted to men of real distinction within a framework that sufficiently limited their power so that they could never arbitrarily oppress their constituents or pursue measures that were disastrous to the community. That the Virginia Convention did not do so well as Carter had hoped was apparent in the years after independence. He was distressed, he wrote in October 1776, that the constitution had not provided for a proper separation between legislative, executive, and judicial powers. "All three powers" seemed to be "crowding to form one tribunal," and the legislature seemed to be usurping all power "according to some democratick, assumed retrospection." Worst of all, as he objected in July 1777, it had failed to stop "the growth of licencious freedom" or to provide against "some sordid self providing creatures, who have been creeping into Legislation by every deception Possible."[116]

Whatever the weaknesses of the Virginia constitution, however, Carter vastly preferred it "to *slavery* and *oppression*" under Great Britain. Indeed, as the war progressed, his antagonism to George III and his followers in both Britain and America increased. "If ever a war began

---

[116] L. C. to Dixon and Hunter, May 1776 (?), Sabine Hall Col.; L. C. to George Washington, Oct. 21, 1776, in Force, ed., *Am. Archives,* 5th Ser., II, 1304–7, and July 30, 1777, Washington Papers, LII, 101.

on the Principles of robbery this did," he declared in February 1777, expressing the hope that "every American" would "dispise every Attempt" at a reconciliation "and forever hug that independency which they have been compelled to, that has thus providentially brought about a Seperation from such a Tyrant, and his adherents." "I every day see more and more of the unhappy base tendency of that G[eorge] 3d," he noted in his diary in April 1777, and for that reason he had no qualms about having disavowed his "allegiance to him." "For my part I think every contract especially about Government is reciprocal with conditions on both sides," he wrote in July 1777; "Allegiance was mine and the condition for it was Justice and freedom together with a Paternal affection. If that is broken or denied me, I am absolved."[117]

That Carter was glad after independence to have been "providentially" separated from Britain did not mean that he had no regrets. It could not have been easy for a man in his mid-sixties who had long prided himself on being an Englishman suddenly to disavow his allegiance and break his emotional ties, and he continued to wonder how Great Britain "in a mere Zenith of trade" with an "empire over almost the whole world" could have so quickly lost its traditional "contempt for Slavery." The answer, he finally decided, was moral decline, the causes of which were "exactly the same" as those that brought about the fall of the Roman Empire, "the only Power to be found in History equal with themselves in extent of dominion." In the case of Rome, the "want of a rival in power (to wit) the destruction of Cathage; brought on all the luxuries and extravagances of trade; so that as by effeminacy and bribery Rome dwindled in freedom, Dic-

---

[117] *L. C. Diary*, Feb. 13, 20, 23, 25, Apr. 20, July 15, 1777, II, pp. 1075, 1078–79, 1082–87, 1096, 1112; L. C. to Purdie, Sept. 1776, Sabine Hall Col.

tators and Emperors grew, mighty; and death, barbarity, Servitude and debauchery, the concomitants of Despotism, Prevailed, to their entire exterpation." Similarly, "Britain, being able by the assistance of her vast Empire, to check, if not Subdue her only rival Powers, France and Spain; and by that means encreasing in trade, instead of Paying off those debts which this successful grasp of empire had occasioned, has run mad with the luxuries of this vast trade; and by sinking into effeminacy and bribery to support that extravagance, have now raised a mere Nero in his despotic inclinations over them." Without some external force to check the natural human tendencies to indolence and evil, nations, like men, seemed to fall into depravity, and more than any other single factor it was the conviction that Britain had degenerated into such a state that seems to have accounted for Carter's joy at having broken the connection. For Landon Carter the American Revolution was a moral drama. With his fellow Americans he was waging a war on corruption, a battle against nothing less than the imperfect nature of man. Such a war was a "noble struggle" indeed, and the ultimate goal was a political utopia on earth: a political society that would embody those values and those ethical imperatives on which he had sought to build a life of virtue.[118]

V Only Inward Satisfaction

Driven into public life by societal demands and his compulsion for distinction, Landon Carter was never completely comfortable there. His uncompromising and stern nature, his insistence upon keeping a proper distance

[118] *L. C. Diary*, Feb. 25, 1777, II, pp. 1085–86.

from men lest too intimate a relationship somehow contaminate him or deprive him of his independence and impartiality, and the extraordinary standards of behavior he demanded from others tended to alienate even his closest associates and thereby precluded the development of strong and enduring friendships and prevented him from ever attaining the warm admiration of the public. Without either, Carter not surprisingly came to feel, especially in his later years, lonely, neglected, and unappreciated. Although he continued as always to pride himself on never having "courted Public applause,"[119] his ego was so great that it required constant feeding. He thought he had done well in life and was proud of his accomplishments as a provider for his family, a planter and man of learning, a public servant, and a virtuous and honorable man. But he was never so sure of the worth of his accomplishments as to be able to scorn completely the opinions of other men—with the result that he constantly demanded reassurance in the form of recognition and respect from his associates. Although he received considerable recognition and no little respect, it was never enough. Puzzled and hurt by the failure of his contemporaries to pay him that regard which he thought his achievements merited, he became so sensitive that the merest slight or the smallest insult sent him scurrying to his plantation and his study for refuge from a hostile and malevolent world. He seems always to have been plagued by a tension deep within him between a sense of responsibility to the public and a desire to retreat to the familiar and friendly privacy of his plantation, by a consuming need for recognition from the outer world and a desire to remain uncorrupted by that world; and his feelings of neglect and his disappointment at having failed to obtain more recognition from his fellowmen during his last decade only accen-

[119] *L. C. Diary*, July 14, 1776, II, p. 1057.

tuated his tendencies toward withdrawal, turning him inward and driving him to seek comfort in his diary and his memories. Lonely, self-pitying, and even a trifle bitter and resentful, he eventually became somewhat paranoiac, willing to suspect everyone—his family, overseers, neighbors, colleagues on the bench—of conspiring to ignore and persecute him. They seemed to have rejected, not only him, but his whole system of values, and his only comfort was the inward satisfaction of knowing that, at least by his standards, he deserved better treatment.

By any standards Carter's accomplishments were impressive, and he was well aware that few of his contemporaries either in Virginia or elsewhere in the English colonies exceeded him in material success. "I cannot help taking notice," he proudly observed in July 1770, of "the care I have taken of my family, the paying off Children's fortunes, and putting out 3 sons with an Estate very well to pass in the world, still maintaining a large family at home," at a cost of about £400 per year, "and all this without being in debt but a very trifle." That debt, which had amounted to around £1,000 in 1766, apparently had been paid off by June 1776, and he could boast in September 1776 that even though Dunmore—"Lord Pilferer"—had robbed him of "a full thousand Pounds in Valuable slaves," he had "many more, besides stocks of all kinds, land Productions not a few, and other reputables (for even a treasury chest) to furnish out a distress." For his extraordinary success he was thankful to God, but he did not underestimate the importance of his own efforts. He could not help but agree with Captain Burgess Ball's estimate in July 1777 that he "was by far the best Planter about," and he had no doubt that "such a success could only be produced by great and sensible experience." Nor was he any less pleased with his public achievements. He was proud, he remarked in March 1774, of his record on the Richmond County court, particularly of the "order and dispatch" he had promoted in the "Publick business" and of the "success in the order an[d] decency I have Preserved in the Co[unty]." During his seventeen years in the House of Burgesses, he could boast to a critic in 1774, he had served his constituents faithfully and diligently without engaging "in any teinted affair," and that service, he declared two years later, had brought him far more "contentment" than was generally "allowed to mankind."[120]

Carter's accomplishments were, moreover, recognized by others. Richard Bland wrote a poem to him in 1758 in which he complimented him on his tracts defending the Burgesses in the pistole fee controversy and pronounced him both his "Country's surest Friend" and "A Friend to Virtue and a Foe to Vice." Lieutenant Governor Francis Fauquier was equally pleased with his various political writings in the early 1760s, and in 1765 Richard Henry Lee addressed him as "one of the best friends, as well as one of the most able of the community." The American Philosophical Society thought his essay on the weevil fly "ingenious and accurate," and on the basis of the same essay Dr. Thomas Bond, the Philadelphia physician, reportedly entertained "the highest opinion of" his "Genius and Abilities" and remarked that the world was "greatly obliged to" him. Even after he had been turned out of the Burgesses, fellow politicians continued to seek his advice, deferring to him as a man of "great Abilities and Experience," of "abilities with good intentions," of "Wisdom and experience." Carter reveled in such tributes, and there is no question, as Francis Lightfoot Lee observed, that he loved "to be tickled." During his first session in the House of Burgesses he took great delight in any

---

[120] *L. C. Diary*, July 6, 1766, July 19, Aug. 18, 1770, Mar. 12, 1771, Sept. 24, 1772, Mar. 1, May 20, 1774, Apr. 9, 1776, July 14, 1777, I, pp. 314–15, 468–69, 548, II, pp. 733, 799, 812–13, 1014–15, 1110–11; L. C. to "My Friend," [Feb. 1774], to Dixon and Hunter, May 1776 (?), and to Purdie, Sept. 1776, Sabine Hall Col.

compliments on his speeches or written addresses. When "Some Gentlemen told" him, "and not a few, so handsome a Speach and so Close an answer they had never met with," he eagerly recorded it in his diary, and on another occasion he thought "the Praise of Everybody and a Vote of the whole house but three" certainly "intitles me to value myself." He received with great relish Dr. Bond's reported praise of his weevil fly essay, and when his nephew Carter Braxton wrote in October 1776 that he would always value Carter's advice because he was a man "whose Experience in Life and Knowledge of Mankind justly entitle him to the Esteem of all admirers of Literature," Carter found it a most "agreeable letter." Carter's love of praise meant, of course, that he was susceptible to flattery. In 1770 Francis Lightfoot Lee wrote to his brother William, who as a tobacco merchant in London was trying to get Carter's business away from his rival, William Molleson, that Molleson kept Carter's loyalty "chiefly by flattery." According to Lee, Molleson "praises" Carter's "writings, publishes them in some London paper, then asks ten thousand pardons, for taking so great a liberty, but his love for mankind obliges him to make them as public as possible." Lee doubted that Carter's consignments were "worth so great a sacrifice."[121]

[121] *L. C. Diary,* Mar. 10, Apr. 15, 1752, Oct. 18, 1774, I, pp. 80, 102, II, p. 880; Fauquier to L. C., June 3, 1760, Miscellaneous Papers, Colonial Williamsburg, Inc.; John Tayloe to L. C., Apr. 26, 1764, Sabine Hall Col.; Richard Lee of Lee Hall to L. C., Mar. 7, 1772, Sept. 20, 1774, Apr. 20, June 9, 1776, Lee-Ludwell Papers, Va. Hist. Soc.; Francis Lightfoot Lee to L. C., Oct. 21, 1775, Jan. 14, 1777, and Carter Braxton to L. C., Oct. 17, 1776, Lee Transcripts, II, 70, 104, IV, 308, Va. Hist. Soc.; Braxton to L. C., Apr. 14, 1776, Fogg Autograph Collection, Maine Historical Society, Portland, Me.; F. L. Lee to William Lee, Apr. 6, 1770, Brock Col., Box 4; R. H. Lee to L. C., June 22, 1765, in Ballagh, ed., *R. H. Lee Letters,* I, 7–8; Richard Bland's poem on L. C., June 20, 1758, in Conway, *Barons of the Potomac and Rappahannock,* 138–41; *Proc. of Am. Phil. Soc.,* XXII (July 1835), Part III, No. 119, 19–20 (Nov. 15, 1768).

But praise did more than simply tickle Carter; it seems to have been essential to his happiness and peace of mind. Respect and attention sustained him; disapproval and neglect threw him into fits of anger and despair. Criticism was almost unbearable. He could not understand, for instance, how "men not remarkt for ever having read more than an adjudged case or two or perhaps than have no other real boast than the making of a Plant of tobacco or two should think themselves at Liberty to criticize" an address he had written for the House of Burgesses when his skill in writing had been so frequently complimented, and his extreme sensitivity to criticism was at the root of most of the violent disputes in which he became involved at one time or another with almost everyone he was ever closely associated with. This inability to accept criticism gracefully was not simply the result of an insufferable arrogance, as some of his contemporaries seem to have thought. He never regarded his own imperfections lightly or considered himself above reproach, but he could see that he had accomplished more than most men and he brooded about the failure or refusal of men of lesser accomplishments to pay him greater deference. The apparent gap between his conception of himself and the way he appeared to others seems to have produced considerable uncertainty within him about the actual importance of his accomplishments, to have raised doubts about his own evaluations of himself; and the only way he could bridge that gap or allay his doubts was to obtain constant reassurance and approval from others. Carter's sensitivity to criticism and dependence upon praise had still other ingredients. There is good evidence to suggest that they were closely related to his failure to match the accomplishments of his father. He had enormous respect for King Carter, who was over fifty when Landon was born and who by 1730 was probably the most commanding figure in Virginia, and his realization that his own achievements, however substantial they might have been, fell far short of those of his father, that he would never make the mark upon his generation that his father had made upon the previous one, and that he would consequently never be accorded that respect and recognition that were given to his father probably caused stirrings of guilt and frustration that were intensified by disapproval and relieved only by praise. In addition, he was so wary of other men, so prone to suspect them of acting with malicious or evil intent, that he could never trust anyone sufficiently to develop a relationship that was close enough to permit easy criticism. Whatever the reasons, Carter seems to have become more and more sensitive with each passing year until by the 1770s the smallest disagreement, the most inconsequential slight, deeply wounded his ego, and he came to regard each of them in turn as a personal affront, a questioning of his abilities, a belittling of his accomplishments, or a direct attack upon his whole structure of values. Much of his world came to seem hostile and ungrateful, and *"Ingratitude"* appeared to him to be no less than *"the Devil,"* "the basis of every species of evil."[122]

The wounds that sank deepest, the instances of ingratitude that hurt the most, were those that came from his family, and particularly from his eldest son Robert Wormeley. What he found most disappointing and most frustrating was his inability to impress his own values and drives upon his children and the apparent rejection by his family of the entire code around which he had built his life. It was becoming clear to him during his last decade that Robert Wormeley had degenerated into a mere "man

---

[122] *L. C. Diary*, Apr. 15, 1752, Sept. 11, 1770, June 25, 1774, Mar. 10, May 12, 1776, I, pp. 102, 487, II, pp. 835–36, 998, 1038–39; *Letter from a Gentleman in Virginia*, 4.

of Pleasure." "He has truely got the name of Wild Bob," he complained in his diary in February 1774, "for there is not one kind of business he cares for but that of gaming and running about." When he did not "moor" himself "to an idle gaming table or figit about from house to house," he either concerned himself with "some trifling imployment" or slept "all day," never seeking to improve his time "now and then in some useful reading or conversation." For Carter, Robert Wormeley's "abandoned devotion" to gaming and pleasure spelled only misfortune and ruin for his family. The "married gamester," Carter lamented in March 1776, "keeps his family in the Perpetual fear of starving," and neither of his sons—John nor Robert Wormeley—seemed to have any sense of family responsibility. Both, he wrote in June 1774, had "wives very big with large gangs of children and yet they play away and play it all away."[123]

Even more serious than the prospect of economic ruin was the possibility of the eventual moral corruption, perhaps even the total decay, of the family. In Carter's opinion the "bad example" set by Robert Wormeley had "murdered" a "fine Genius" in his son Landon. Carter had already begun to suspect by the early 1770s that unless Robert Wormeley drastically altered his behavior young Landon would "in a very little time become the most outrageous of all children that ever lived" and would eventually revenge "the ill usage I have ever received from his Parent," and by the middle 1770s these suspicions were well on the way to being confirmed. Young Landon's stay at the College of William and Mary in 1772 and 1773 only further "improved his talk for triflings and loungings," and by September 1774 no amount of persua-

---

[123] *L. C. Diary*, Sept. 28, 1770, Feb. 12, June 16, 1774, Mar. 13, 16, May 9, July 26, 1776, I, p. 505, II, pp. 795, 830, 1000–1001, 1004, 1036, 1064.

sion could induce him to give up "one moment" of his pleasure. "Like father like Son," Carter despaired in March 1776; "I wonder everybody can't go to hell by themselves without endeavouring to carry his Children there." Soon, he predicted in February 1774, neither son nor grandson would be any better than "the rest of mankind, some of whom are but Idiots." For the principal heir in two successive generations thus to forsake distinction for dissipation could only result "in an intire mortification" of the family and it would not, he feared, take "many generations to compleat the Catastrophe."[124]

Carter did not sit idly by and watch the degeneration of his family. His concern for its welfare, his conception of himself as its conscience—the one shield against its almost certain corruption—and his refusal ever to be content with failure drove him to try every means at his disposal, reason, cajolery, threats, demands, special favors, to dissuade Robert Wormeley from pursuing his destructive habits, to persuade him to recognize the necessity of closely adhering to his own rigid structure of values. "God send that those who wait for my estate may wait long enough," he prayed in December 1774, "for I would willingly save a Soul or two alive before I die," and he vowed to his grandson at that time that he "never would give over striving to save him whilst under my roof." But his repeated and more or less perpetual campaigns for the salvation of his son and grandson seemed only to increase their defiance and produced in Carter acute frustration and a suspicion that Robert Wormeley did things deliberately because "he knows it fluxes me" and was "fond of torturing his father." When company came, Robert Wormeley endeavored "to get

[124] *L. C. Diary,* June 16, 1771, June 25, 1772, June 29, 1773, Feb. 12, Sept. 14, 1774, Mar. 10, 13, 1776, I, pp. 577–78, II, pp. 702, 765, 795, 857–58, 998, 1000–1001.

78

them to Cards" so that Carter could not have "a word's conversation of any one of them," and at dinner he picked "out all titbits, then asks everybody to have them and at last asks his father." Robert Wormeley refused even to admit that Carter was "a tollerable manager" of his plantations. "Every thing that I do must be excessively wrong," Carter complained in July 1770, "although vastly superior in the produce to any proportion of his profit and much greater than better lands have produced for any number of years in my Neighbourhood." He finally came to regard Robert Wormeley as his "most vexatious tyrant," and what disturbed him the more was that "everybody" seemed "to take a Pleasure that he is so." Such "species of filial disrespect," such evident ingratitude, were to Carter "past all bearing," and by March 1776 he was ready to believe that Robert Wormeley would put him "out of the way" if the law did not "Prevent Parricide." "Good God," he declared in his diary, "that such a monster should have descended from my loins."[125]

How justified Carter's reactions were, how accurately they caught the spirit and intent of his son's behavior, is now impossible to tell. Certainly, Robert Wormeley had ample provocation; Carter's insistence upon constantly "advising" a mature man could have driven anyone to take reprisals. He seemed unable to understand, as Robert Wormeley reminded him in March 1776, that a "40 year old man . . . was not a child to be controuled," arrogantly insisting that even "40 ought to hear reasons" and having complete confidence that his reason and experience were superior to those of his son. Carter undoubtedly believed that he was "a kind, an indulgent and an humane Parent," but he demanded a standard of conduct that few

[125] *L. C. Diary*, July 19, 1770, Oct. 3, 1772, Aug. 12, Dec. 24–25, 1774, Feb. 15–16, Mar. 16, 1776, I, pp. 447–48, II, pp. 736, 848–49, 902–4, 983–84, 1004.

men could meet. It is also probable that Carter's extreme sensitivity to criticism and disagreement caused him to misinterpret many innocent acts and remarks as insult and disrespect and that he tended to magnify such things on the part of his son, to find them all the harder to bear, because they stood in such stark contrast to the great regard he had always held for his own father. But whatever the causes and nature of the storms at Sabine Hall, there is no question that to Carter they were much more than minor domestic spats. He was convinced both that his son was deliberately disrespectful and that he had rejected almost everything he had stood for, and this belief wounded him deeply and caused him repeated anguish and bewilderment. He seemed unable to push it out of his consciousness. It became the dominant theme in his diary, and he even came to conceive of the diary as a record of the "evident misconduct" and "extraordinary manouvres" of his son. He continued to hope for a change in his son's behavior. But his hopes were in vain. There was no apology, no reconciliation, no amendment by Robert Wormeley. "I have tried every way to be better treated," he lamented in August 1774, "but cannot even Purchase it of him; many are the Pounds that I have paid out of my Pocket for him; but nothing will do."[126]

Frustrated at his inability to effect a reformation in his son and puzzled how to account for such ingratitude and disrespect, Carter searched everywhere for explanations. One obvious cause was Robert Wormeley's constant attachment to gaming, his fondness for keeping company with "Pernicious . . . Gamesters and Spendthrifts; who by taking no care, are reducing themselves, whilst I am keeping as well as I can, my buckle and thong together."

[126] *L. C. Diary*, June 23, 1773, Aug. 12, 1774, Sept. 18, 1775, Feb. 15–16, Mar. 9, 15, Apr. 3, 1776, II, pp. 762–63, 848–49, 944–45, 983–84, 997–98, 1001–2, 1009–10.

But the primary cause Carter finally fixed upon was the "Princesslike art" of Robert Wormeley's wife, Winifred Travers Beale. To Carter, at least in his declining years, most women were Eve figures who had, as he remarked in August 1772, "nothing in the general in view, but the breeding contests at home." "I don't think there can be a more treacherous, interprising, Perverse, and hellish Genius than is to be met with in A Woman," he declared in April 1777 in reponse to a report that some Philadelphia ladies had tried to help the British by spiking American guns; "Madam Eve we see at the very hazard of Paradise suffered the devil to tempt her; and of such a tendency has her sex been." Nor did any woman have any more "of the devil" in her than his daughter-in-law. She was the epitome of the temptress, and she was largely responsible for the "prodigeous vein of contradiction" in Robert Wormeley. "I have had 3 women to wife," he declared in July 1777, "but never one of them, like Lady Fat, [a] Lady for lying and scolding, and thus it is I do suppose, by the husband's warping to her temper has he turned a mere bulldog." Furthermore, Carter suspected that she might even have been part of the conspiracy with her father William Beale and her brother Reuben that resulted in Reuben's marriage to Carter's daughter Judith against Carter's express wishes. The whole Beale family, in fact, seemed to be endeavoring by some "concealed . . . scheme" to persecute Carter by ruining his children. Never taking "any care to educate their own" and seeing "others exceeding them," they tried, Carter charged in December 1774, purely "out of revenge . . . every treachery to decoy young people off from Duty." "I never knew many of them possessed with any justice or Principle," he wrote in his diary in June 1773, and their "hellish machinations" only confirmed him in his judgment that it was "as necessary to consult the Pedigree of men and women, as it is that of

Mules and horses. A good breed of either must be great riches."[127]

It was not only the machinations of his daughter-in-law and her family and the disrespect of Robert Wormeley that Carter had to endure. His overseers became so impudent and disrespectful that they deliberately disobeyed his "express orders" and tried to tell him how to run his own plantations. Even in his own house no one followed his directions or tried to take "the least care of any one thing." By September 1775 he could only conclude that there was a general "Combination against" him that extended over his entire plantation. Even more difficult to bear was the neglect of his children and grandchildren in his declining years. "Everybody," he ruefully concluded in April 1777, "is for themselves." His daughters visited him only infrequently and never stayed very long, and his grandchildren were not even grateful enough to keep him company when he was "alone" in his "extreme age and great infirmity." "In virginia," he complained in November 1763, "a man dyes a month sooner in a fit of any disorders because he can't have one soul to talk to. If he has children some are one way and some another. And without a wife, who has a sick man to converse with?" "It is a pity," he lamented in September 1772, "that old age . . . should be so contemptible in the eyes of the world" that even the children of "the aged" seemed "to despise them." "Some few," he thought, "fancy they ought to behave otherwise, and do so in the main, but not amongst my really ungrateful children," and he was thankful that his "limbs as yet" served him "to ride out" and his "eyes by the help of glasses" enabled him "to read and dispise them in my turn." Indeed, things had gotten to

[127] *L. C. Diary*, Aug. 18, Oct. 3, 1772, June 23, 1773, Aug. 12, Oct. 5, Dec. 21, 1774, Apr. 27, July 7, 1777, II, pp. 713, 736, 762–63, 848–49, 865, 900, 1103, 1106–7.

such a pitch that he even came to think, as he declared in April 1772, that "families desired their old Parents to die."[128]

Had Carter had more esteem and approval from the public, the neglect and disrespect of his family might not have weighed so heavily on his mind, but ingratitude seemed to have taken hold of his whole world. In September 1772 his friend, lawyer Richard Parker, insulted him openly in court, and, though he later made a public apology, Carter could only infer from the event that "with some people no Person nor behaviour can be intitled to a decent respect." "I have been a slave to everybody in the County," he reflected after the incident, "and yet without either Severity or arbitrariness in my behaviour nor anything but a resolution to do my duty, I am the most insulted of any man in it." In response to the report that Dr. Bond had said that Carter's pamphlet on the weevil fly had "immortalized" him and that "all Europe" had "actually addressed" him "upon it" and so venerated him "as to Pronounce" him "the greatest Natural Philosopher of this age" with "almost Universal knowledge," Carter wrote in his diary that "if the Gent has preserved the truth I may say that in me is verified the saying that A Prophet is not without honour save in his own Country; for here I publish my discoveries on the Weavil fly, and it was hardly so much noticed, as to encourage but here and there a sensible gentleman to experience its good effects." Though he later decided when the reported address failed to appear that Dr. Bond must be "either a talker or a deceiver," he had hoped the report was true because, as he remarked when he first heard it, it would have given

---

[128] *L. C. Diary*, Apr. 25, 1758, Nov. 23, 1763, Apr. 6, Sept. 2, 1772, Sept. 9, 1773, Oct. 6, Dec. 30, 1774, Sept. 21, 1775, Apr. 17, July 14, 1777, I, pp. 221–22, 242, II, pp. 668, 720, 767–68, 866–67, 907, 947, 1092, 1110–11.

him great happiness in his old age to see his "endeavour to serve mankind so generally acknowledged." But Carter was never to receive the kind of acknowledgment he craved so much, and the ingratitude of his country preyed heavily upon his mind. The best he could hope for was that, as he wrote in March 1774, "however disrespected by many about," he would be wanted after his death "by many people who may now wish me gone" to help check "a prodigeous stride to a Lawless behaviour" that he saw arising in the country. "I often think of the old Roman who received every disgrace untill he was drove from his Country," he wrote in February 1776, "and yet when ignorance brought those who insulted him into a state of dispair, he alone was capable Of and did reprove them and again reinstated that happiness which they had lost."[129]

But such hopes were small comfort, especially when after independence Carter was deprived even of the credit for his greatest moment in history, his attack in the fall of 1764 upon Parliament's proposed stamp duties and his role in persuading the House of Burgesses to send petitions of protest to the King, Lords, and Commons at that time. He was disturbed to learn in July 1776 that Governor Patrick Henry, who had, of course, been instrumental in pushing the famed Virginia resolutions against the Stamp Act through the House of Burgesses in May 1765, had been credited at the Virginia Convention with being "the first who opened the breath of liberty to America." Carter was pleased that it had been "with truth replied, and Proved that that breath was first breathed and supported by a person not then taken notice of," but, although he claimed the merit accorded to Henry for him-

[129] *L. C. Diary,* Sept. 9, 11, 1772, Mar. 1, Oct. 18, 1774, Feb. 6, 1776, II, pp. 726–27, 799, 880, 976; Richard Lee to L. C., Sept. 20, 1776, Apr. 20, 1776, Lee-Ludwell Papers.

self, he was proud, he wrote in his diary, that he had never, like Henry, "courted Public applause; and if any endeavour assists my country, I care not who enjoys the merit of it." Rather than participatè in any schemes of popularity, he preferred to do "without honour" from "his own country," convinced that "virtue will ever carry its own reward." Despite his professions, however, Carter was especially bothered by this incident, and it came to serve as a symbol of his failure to receive that respect, gratitude, and recognition he was convinced were rightfully his.[130]

For six months after the incident he was seeking reassurances, first from Francis Lightfoot Lee, then from George Washington and probably from others that he really had been "first, in *America*," to attack the Parliamentary vote "to tax the Colonies with certain stamp duties" and that Henry had not even been at that assembly but had "only assisted in the resolves after the stamp act came in." To see another receive the distinction for so signal an honor as being the first to protest "such an unconstitutional stretch of Power in . . . Parliament" was scarcely bearable. He was proud to have played a role like Cato's in spiriting his countrymen up to a defense of their freedom, but it was unjust and painful to be deprived of Cato's just reward, the reward of "never" being "forgotten." Finally, in September 1776 Carter was driven to assert in a public essay his claim of being "uncontrovertably the first admonisher of this impending combined despotism, in a memorable as well as Public Assembly." Though his many "instances of duty" to society had been "so remarkably requited with a disregard," he had faith, he told the public, that "the God who assists the 13 united States of America, in maintaining

---

[130] *L. C. Diary*, July 14, 1776, II, p. 1057.

their Just claims" would "not desert a faithful servant to mankind though now something enfeebled with Years," and in the meantime he would "injoy a comfort in even a Conscious (though Unattended) *Merui.*" "*Haec, ego Primus tentavi*" (I was the first to try this), he concluded his essay, "*tulis alter honorem*" (but another received the honors). Though it included the characteristic scorn of public applause, this essay was in essence a plea for public recognition, but it obviously failed in its intent and Carter continued to brood about the refusal of the public to appreciate his important contribution to the Revolutionary movement. In February 1777 when William Dennis, a British ship captain temporarily interned in the neighborhood, displayed some talent at making portraits in "Chalk and Charcoal," Carter persuaded him to "take" his "figure" and he "produced a serious, thoughtful old gentleman holding in his right hand a paper thus inscribed: America, Freedom supported Against the British Stamp Act. *Merui, sed intus tantum fruor.*" The Latin "motto" meant, "in spite of my merit, I have only inward satisfaction," and Carter, as he explained in his diary, intended it to allude "to the evident ingratitude of others as to him who first opened this door to freedom, to leave him [on]ly the inner satisfaction as a rewa[rd]."[131]

Carter's growing conviction that the only reward one might expect on earth was inward satisfaction only intensified what appears to have been a life-long tendency toward withdrawal. Uncomfortable with other men and afraid that too close a contact with a corrupt world would somehow stain his virtue, he seems to have been devoted to the ideal of his plantation as a rural retreat where he might enjoy a life of quiet meditation and uncorrupted virtue on the Horatian model. He named his house Sabine

---

[131] *L. C. Diary,* July 25, 1776, Feb. 23–24, 1777, II, pp. 1063, 1082–84; L. C. to Purdie, Sept. 1776, Sabine Hall Col.; L. C. to Washington, Oct. 21, 1776, in Force, ed., *Am. Archives,* 5th Ser., II, 1304–7.

Hall after Horace's sheltered "Sabine vale" in the hills behind Rome where, as Horace wrote in his poem "Contentment," he could expect to live undisturbed by the rush for "fame," and "worth," and "Praise," away from the "doubled wealth and doubled care" of Rome.[132] Carter seems to have found unusually congenial the central character's advice in Joseph Addison's play *Cato* always to retreat from "a corrupted state"

> To thy paternal seat, the Sabine field
> Where the great Censor toiled with his own hands,
> And all our frugal ancestors were blessed
> In humble virtues, and a rural life.
> There live retired, pray for the peace of Rome:
> Content thyself to be obscurely good.
> When vice prevails, and impious men bear sway,
> The post of honor is a private station.[133]

Whenever politics took a turn he could not sanction, he always declared his intention to retire, as he declared in 1776, to his "Private station" at Sabine Hall: "This only Post of honour." Thus, according to Richard Bland, he decided for reasons not now entirely clear to withdraw from public life in 1758 after two terms in the House of Burgesses, professing that he would "envy not . . . the great,"

Their Pomp, their Luxury, their pageant state,
But bless'd with all that Heav'n below can give
A mind contented and a taste to live,
[He'd] . . . smile superior on their empty show,
Their seeming pleasure and their real woe
At Sabine Hall, retir'd from public praise,
[He'd] . . . spend in learned ease [his] . . . future days.

Similarly, in 1765 he thought it better "to retire and lament in private" rather than to be "publickly . . . concerned" as a burgess in consenting to reduce his country

---

[132] "Of Contentment," conveniently in Francis R. B. Godolphin, ed., *The Latin Poets* (New York, 1949), 256.

[133] Act IV, scene 4, ll. 140–51.

to slavery by submitting to the Stamp Act, and in the months after Lexington and Concord he not only threatened but actually did withdraw "from public business," giving up his lieutenancy for the county because of his objections to the provisions for court martials in a new militia law and quitting the county court because the people were "Poisoned by . . . Popularity." Despite a sincere desire to withdraw entirely from the public arena, it was hard for Carter to bring himself to do it. His devotion to public service was too intense and his ambition to win distinction by meritoriously serving the community was too great. Both in 1758 and 1765 he ran for reelection and won, justifying his decision to stay in public life on the grounds that his resignation might bring an inferior man to office or, as Francis Lightfoot Lee wrote in urging him not to retire in 1775, that if he could not "do all the good" he "could wish" he could "at least endeavour to prevent all the mischief in" his power. Even after he had left the court in 1775 and vowed never to return he did resume his commission in 1777, unable to resist a plea by a "worthy member" for him to "come to give weight and order to the Proceedings." When he did leave the Burgesses in 1768 it was because he was turned out by the voters, and even his semiretirement after 1775 could be attributed, as Carter himself inferred in 1776, not to his own decision but to his inability to get along with the younger men in the county, an inability he preferred to attribute to "something factious and imperious in the sway of mankind."[134]

[134] *L. C. Diary,* May 9, 1774, Sept. 4, 1775, Feb. 6, 1776, Apr. 7, Aug. 8, 1777, II, pp. 808, 937, 976, 1089, 1121; Richard Bland's poem on L. C., June 20, 1758, in Conway, *Barons of the Potomac and Rappahannock,* 138–41; R. H. Lee to L. C., June 22, 1765, in Ballagh, ed., *R. H. Lee Letters,* I, 7–8; L. C. to Joseph Royle, June 3, 1765, Brock Col.; Francis Lightfoot Lee to L. C., Oct. 21, 1775, Lee Transcripts, II, 70, Va. Hist. Soc.; L. C. to Dixon and Hunter, May 1776 (?), Sabine Hall Col.

But Carter's gradual retirement to a "Private station" after he was turned out of the House of Burgesses in 1768 did not—because of his passion for distinction, could not—bring him the contentment he had wished for. Rather, it only afforded him more time to fret over the ingratitude and disrespect that seemed to be his portion in life and that had been at least in part responsible for driving him out of public life. With time "heavy on his hands" and constantly at odds with most of the members of his family, he turned more and more to his diary for comfort and asylum and there repeatedly speculated about the causes of his distress. Simple envy of his "good Estate" and his general success in life, he thought, was in part responsible, as was his age, which, given the universal "practice of moderns . . . of worshiping the rising sun and disregarding the setting," made it impossible to merit "anything from the rising generation." He even entertained the possibility that there might be no such thing as real gratitude, that esteem might be no more than "a Species of love not really merited," a "passion that enslaves the mind without . . . conviction." What did not occur to him, however, was that the primary reason why he failed to win the admiration and respect of his contemporaries might have been his strict devotion—to the exclusion of any other considerations—to those values on which he sought to build a life of virture, values that served not only as a shield to protect him from the public's hostility but also as a barrier that deprived him of its love. Whenever it came to a choice, he preferred to rely upon his "good conscience" for "shelter" rather than upon the esteem of the public, to be respected because of his integrity rather than to be loved, because, like Speaker John Robinson, he "was a jewil of a man." To adhere to his code, to avoid offending his own conscience, to know he had done what was right and good, were more important to Carter than the feelings or respect of any man. At least in part, then, he failed to win the praise of the public because he had succeeded too well in keeping to his personal values. He attained a large measure of that praiseworthiness he coveted so much only at the sacrifice of the praise that he seemed to need so badly. To be sure, he derived some comfort in "being but now and then obscurely good" in his "Private station"—in the inward satisfaction he derived from knowing that he merited more than he received. But few men take comfort in knowing they deserve more than they receive, and Landon Carter appears to have done so least of all.[135]

VI   *Epilogue*

Like every other man, Landon Carter was, of course, sui generis. No other man before, during, or after his lifetime has ever had *precisely* the same structure of personality, arrangement of character traits, and psychological needs and drives; encountered *exactly* the same problems; or reacted to them in *exactly* the same way as he. He could, of course, be placed within any general system of psychological types and, if materials were available for comparable analyses of his contemporaries, within one of the half-dozen or so dominant social types into which the male members of the Virginia gentry could probably be divided. Both because it would be methodologically unsound and because it would conflict sharply with other existing evidence, it would obviously not, however, be

---

[135] *L. C. Diary,* Sept. 11, Oct. 9, 1772, Mar. 1, Dec. 13, 21, 1774, June 17, 1775, Feb. 6, Mar. 8, July 25, 1776, Feb. 23, July 8, 1777, II, pp. 727, 738, 799, 895–96, 900, 923, 976, 996, 1063, 1082–83, 1109; L. C.'s reply to poem, Nov. 1, 1768, and L. C. to Dixon and Hunter, May 1776 (?), Sabine Hall Col.

either possible or desirable to argue that Carter's individual psychology and the collective psychology of the gentry were in any comprehensive sense isomorphic, that any precise correspondence could be established between them.

What can and must be argued, however, is that Carter's particular code of behavior and psychological drives make him an excellent, and, in all probability, highly reliable, guide to the value structure of the gentry as a whole. For one thing, his extreme self-consciousness and his habit of committing his thoughts to writing caused him to give explicit expression to commonplace ideas and assumptions that men less introspective and less preoccupied with and sensitive to the causes and implications of their own behavior would have taken for granted. More important, because distinction necessarily requires public recognition and because such recognition comes only to those who have behaved in accordance with those rules of conduct that the public recognizes as desirable, Carter's compulsive quest for distinction, his assiduous cultivation of those values to which he thought it was neccessary to adhere in order to achieve distinction, makes him a peculiarly appropriate subject for the study of the individual values and social imperatives of his peers among the gentry—the group which by virtue of its social position determined in large measure the standards for approved behavior in colonial and Revolutionary Virginia. Carter's career, in fact, pointedly demonstrates just how powerful those values and imperatives could be, to what an extraordinary extent they could shape individual behavior. Unlike many other public men who find themselves caught in a perpetual dialectic between their own private impulses and the accepted values of society, Carter achieved a remarkable degree of unity between his interior and exterior worlds by internalizing the imperatives of his society so completely that they became actual character traits. Of course, his obvious discomfort in public life and his failure ultimately to secure the kind of respect and acclaim he thought he deserved make it clear that the values he represented were the *ideal* values of the gentry—the rules its members thought men should live by— rather than the values many of them actually did live by. Through Carter's discomforts and disappointments, however, one can gain as well some understanding of the *actual* values—the customary modes of day-to-day behavior—of the gentry, the nature and extent of the discrepancies between the ideal and the actual, and the severe tensions that could be produced in men as a result of those discrepancies. By driving Carter inside himself, these same discomforts and disappointments seem to have been in large part responsible for his keeping the type of diary that provides the virtually unique materials that speak to all of these problems, make it possible for a later generation of Americans to see in operation the ideals and principles upon which he and his group relied to help give structure and purpose to their lives, and, ironically, assure Landon Carter of a special kind of place in history that will forever be denied his more successful and more applauded contemporaries.

Index

Moderation, 21-28
Molleson, William, London merchant, 74
Money, paper, 7, 41
Muse, Hudson (d. 1799), as delegate to 1776 Convention, 65

Nassau, slave, drinking, 18
Newspapers, 9, 19; see also *Maryland Gazette* and *Virginia Gazettes*
Nicholas, Robert Carter (1728-80), on Townshend duties, 58
North, Lord, *see* Guilford
Northern Neck, holdings in, 3-5
Northumberland Co.: holdings in, 3; Carter manages land in, 2

Old Place, plantation, 3
Ordinary, 23
Overseers, 29, 38; Carter's opinion of, 13

Page family, relation to, 3
Paine, Thomas (1736-1809), author, 9, 61-62; *see also* Independence from Britain *and Common Sense*
Paper Currency Act of 1758, Carter defends, 7
Parker, Richard (1729-1813), lawyer, 83
Parliament, British: fallibility of, 15; powers of, 27, 50-53, 59; Tea Act, 17, 57, 63; Townshend Acts, 54-55, 58; *see also* Stamp Act crisis
Parsons, *see* Clergy
Patriotism, 48
Pendleton, Edmund (1721-1803): burgess, 7; on Townshend Acts, 58
Pistole fee dispute, 41; Carter's role in, 7, 48, 73

Play, Carter's opinion of, 23
Plows and plowing, Carter's opinion of, 29
Political theories, Carter's 40-70
Pope, Alexander (1688-1744), author, 21
Popularity, 46-48, 63-66
Prince William Co., holdings in, 5
Publications and writings, Carter's, 9, 17, 31-33, 73-74; agricultural, 32, 33-34, 73, 83; philosophical, 20-21; political, 7-8, 9, 17, 19, 22, 26-27, 32-33, 35, 41-42, 43, 45-46, 49-51, 66-67, 85-86; scientific, 8, 24
Public service: importance of, 33-35; neglected, 56
Purdie, Alexander (d. 1790), printer, 17, 35, 39; letter to, 59

Races, 23
Randolph, John, Jr. (1728-84), visits Carter, 24
Randolph, Peyton (1721-75): accompanies Carter to play, 23; burgess, 7
Rappahannock River, 3, 5
Reason, 20-21
Rector Detected, 18, 19, 27, 43, 45
Religion, 37-38; *see also* Church *and* Clergy
Republicanism, 63-68
Reynolds, George, leveling sentiments, 65
Richmond Co.: and American Revolution, 8; burgesses, 6-7; Committee of Safety, 63-64; delegates to 1776 Convention, 65; elections, 65; free school for, 30; holdings in, 3-4, 5;

97